Praise for *On Ben*

If you long for a more effective prayer life, this study is for you. *On Bended Knee* will guide you through the prayers of biblical prophets, warriors, and kings—and you'll learn the secrets of talking to God, seeking His wisdom, and getting results! This study is filled with profound teaching, thought-provoking questions, and action steps that produce positive change. Crickett Keeth's teaching will capture your heart and lead you into an intimate relationship with God. Gather a group of friends and take your prayer life to a deeper level.

CAROL KENT, speaker and author, *He Holds My Hand: Experiencing God's Presence and Protection*

Crickett Keeth is a passionate guide as she leads you to study some of the most meaningful and heartfelt prayers found in Scripture. Her thought-provoking questions encourage you to look upward, deeper, and reflectively on the prayers of prophets, warriors, and kings. *On Bended Knee* will bless and challenge you to bend your knee in a fresh way.

CYNTHIA HEALD, author of the Becoming a Woman Bible study series and *Drawing Near to the Heart of God*

I'm so thankful for this much needed study on prayer. Crickett has done a beautiful job parsing the many facets of prayer and laying the pieces in front of us so we can better understand and apply this most intimate part of our relationship with Christ. Dividing the study into heartfelt prayer themes, such as intercession, longing, lament, boldness, and more gives us starting points since prayer can often be overwhelming. You'll also love studying the prayers of men and women in Scripture from whom we get our greatest prayer examples. If you're looking to deepen your prayer life, pick up this study and gather a group of friends together!

KELLY MINTER, Bible teacher and author of *No Other Gods* and *Wherever the River Runs*

Crickett Keeth is a woman of prayer, and this study is a beautiful guide for those wanting to be people who pray. She humbly leads the way with her knees bent and eyes fixed on Jesus.

ELLIE HOLCOMB, Dove Award winning singer/songwriter

On Bended Knee is an inspiring study that not only increased my knowledge of prayer, but more importantly, moved my heart as it convicted me to examine my own prayer life and see what needs to be changed. It is the perfect blend of thought-provoking questions, challenging quotes, and the author's honest and transparent reflections that I found myself relating to again and again. What a refreshing study of what prayer should look like!

RACHEL PRUETT, Women's Ministry Director at Denton Bible Church, Denton, TX

Most Christians find it difficult to pray at times. Even the most practiced do. I don't need a designer approach for staying on my knees. I need biblical conditioning and encouragement. *On Bended Knee* is a godsend that keeps sending us back to God in prayer.

COLE HUFFMAN, Senior Pastor at First Evangelical Church, Memphis, TN

Reading *On Bended Knee* reminded me of how welcoming God is. Imagine! God Himself inviting us to talk to Him about anything, everything, without pretense or reserve. Thank you, Crickett, for writing so honestly and vulnerably about prayer. While I found myself digging into the Scriptures and gaining new insights from this study, the best thing I can say about it is that I kept closing it because all I wanted to do was pray.

JAN WINEBRENNER, author of *The Grace of Catastrophe* and *Intimate Faith*

Crickett Keeth is my favorite Bible study writer. As she always does, in her work *On Bended Knee*, she weds timeless truths of Scripture with timely application. She has this gift for talking about theological insights in a way that makes readers feel as if she's sitting with us at the kitchen table. And we find we are changed. I highly recommend her work for both group and individual use.

SANDRA GLAHN, author of the Coffee Cup Bible Study series; Interim Chair and Associate Professor of Media Arts and Worship at Dallas Theological Seminary

Who doesn't want a deeper prayer life? Then, what better place to turn than to biblical characters who poured out their hearts to God—in times of despair, longing, lament, seeking, dependence and boldness. How providential that a resource such as Crickett Keeth's new Bible study *On Bended Knee* is now available. This seasoned Bible teacher deftly examines the lives of Jesus, Paul, Job, Hannah, David and others in order for us to better understand how prayer can change a life. I love that Crickett is both deep and practical. As she takes us through the study, we are prompted with provocative questions and application for our own lives—while at the same time being encouraged with wisdom from history's great prayer warriors. Throughout, she keeps our focus in prayer on the Lord and pursuing His will and His way in all things. I highly recommend *On Bended Knee* for either personal or group study.

LUCINDA SECREST MCDOWELL, author of *Ordinary Graces* and *Dwelling Places*

Prayer nourishes our relationship with God. Without it we shrivel up and die spiritually. But too often today's frenzied pace beguiles us while we silently starve. Biblically sound and thoroughly practical, *On Bended Knee* will transform your appetite to commune with your eagerly awaiting Father. Invite some friends, pull up a chair, and savor this nutritious biblical feast that will invigorate and sustain your prayer life. Taste and see that prayer is good.

SUE EDWARDS, author of the Discover Together Bible Study series; Associate Professor of Educational Ministries and Leadership at Dallas Theological Seminary

Do you sometimes wonder how to pray effectively? Do you wonder how to approach God with your concerns? If so, you'll appreciate *On Bended Knee*. This eight-week Bible study will lead you into a deeper understanding of prayer as a pathway to intimacy with God and a privilege that contains the power to change the world. Whether you use it for your own personal study or within a group setting, you'll enjoy its easy-to-follow format packed with biblical truth, personal application questions, and inspirational quotes by great Christian leaders.

GRACE FOX, author of *Moving from Fear to Freedom: A Woman's Guide to Peace in Every Situation*, international speaker, global worker

ON BENDED KNEE

PRAYING LIKE PROPHETS, WARRIORS, AND KINGS

—

CRICKETT KEETH

MOODY PUBLISHERS

CHICAGO

Edited by Amanda Cleary Eastep
Interior Design: Erik M. Peterson
Cover Design: Dean Renninger
Cover illustration of brush strokes copyright © 2018 by wacomka / Shutterstock (662769085). All rights reserved.
Author Photo: Nancy B. Webb Photography

Library of Congress Cataloging-in-Publication Data
Names: Keeth, Crickett., author.
Title: On bended knee : praying like prophets, warriors, and kings / Crickett Keeth.
Description: Chicago : Moody Publishers, [2019] | Includes bibliographical references.
Identifiers: LCCN 2019003395 (print) | LCCN 2019009825 (ebook) | ISBN 9780802497888 () | ISBN 9780802419194
Subjects: LCSH: Bible--Prayers. | Prayer--Biblical teaching--Textbooks.
Classification: LCC BS680.P64 (ebook) | LCC BS680.P64 .K44 2019 (print) | DDC 248.3/2--dc23
LC record available at https://lccn.loc.gov/2019003395

ISBN: 978-0-8024-1919-4

We hope you enjoy this book from Moody Publishers. Our goal is to provide high-quality, thought-provoking books and products that connect truth to your real needs and challenges. For more information on other books and products written and produced from a biblical perspective, go to www.moodypublishers.com or write to:

Moody Publishers
820 N. LaSalle Boulevard
Chicago, IL 60610

3 5 7 9 10 8 6 4

Printed in the United States of America

This book is dedicated in loving memory to my mom, Marjorie Jones Keeth. She taught me how to pray as a little girl and continued to model prayer until her final days on this earth. Mom wrote these words to us later in life:

Conduct yourself in a manner that is pleasing to God by loving others, put God first in your life, learn to forgive and forget, control your tongue, be humble, have a right attitude, and last, but not least, pray to God and thank Him every day for all the blessings He has given you.

She left a legacy of eternal significance. Thank you, Mom, for always pointing me to Jesus!

CONTENTS

HOW TO MAKE THE MOST OF THIS STUDY

I'm so glad you have chosen to go through this Bible study, *On Bended Knee*. Each time I study these prayers, God shows me ways I can strengthen my own prayer life. I pray you will see the same result in your life.

Some questions will be easy as you're asked to write down observations from the passage. But there will also be questions that go beyond simple answers—questions that will challenge you and make you ponder the answer. Don't get discouraged if you're not sure how to answer. The purpose of these questions is to move you to deeper study of the passage and promote rich discussion in small groups. With the more challenging questions, try to answer them on your own first before looking at a commentary or study Bible.

I wrote this study to help deepen my own intimacy with God in prayer—wanting to go beyond just saying words and going through the motions to praying with heartfelt honesty to the One I can trust completely. As you study and see the heart behind these prayers, my desire is that you would pray in a way you've not prayed before and that you would experience a deeper intimacy with God as a result.

Each week's lesson provides five days of study. Each day contains four sections, including:

Looking to God's Word directs you to the Scripture for that day, guiding you through observation and interpretation questions.

Looking Upward challenges you to wrestle with thought-provoking questions and promotes group discussion.

Looking Deeper encourages you to look at additional passages that will deepen your study.

Looking Reflectively focuses on application and reflection of the lesson.

To get the most out of this study, take time each day to do a lesson and reflect on the passage and main thought(s), allowing God's Spirit to speak to you and work in you through His Word.

Ask God to teach you, through the study of His Word, how to pray from the heart like these prophets, warriors, and kings.

PRAYING LIKE PROPHETS, WARRIORS, AND KINGS: AN INTRODUCTION

E. M. Bounds, in his book *Purpose in Prayer*, challenges us concerning how we spend time in prayer. He wrote, "Prayer is not a meaningless function or duty to be crowded into the busy or the weary ends of the day, and we are not obeying our Lord's command when we content ourselves with a few minutes upon our knees in the morning rush or late at night when the faculties, tired with the tasks of the day, call out for rest . . . we can never get to know Him if we use the vehicle of prayer as we use the telephone—for a few words of hurried conversation."[1]

When I first read these words, they convicted me because some days my prayers are hurried. Other days, I feel I'm just going through a routine, but not thinking about my relationship with the One to whom I'm praying.

I knew my prayer life wasn't what it needed to be (and I'm still growing in this area). That's why I wrote this Bible study—to learn how to go deeper in prayer by studying the prayers of men and women in the Bible. This study looks at the heart behind the prayers. How did they approach God? What motivated them to pray? How did they pray? How did their relationship with God deepen as a result of their prayers? I wanted to learn how to pray by "listening" to these men and women pray.

You may be wondering why I chose the title *On Bended Knee: Praying Like Prophets, Warriors, and Kings*. I want my prayers to go deeper than just asking God to give me something or "bless me." I want to pray like these men and women we're going to be studying—prophets who were committed to God's truth and pointed others to Him; warriors who fought not only in physical battles with armor and swords, but prayer warriors who fought for God's will to be done; and kings who faced overwhelming situations they knew they couldn't handle on their own.

Today, we can identify with each of these characters regarding what moved them to prayer and how we can pray in similar circumstances.

As I studied their prayers, it was clear these people of God weren't just saying words. They were pouring out their hearts to the One they knew is sovereign. They knew He could strengthen them when they were weak; He could guide them when they didn't know which way to turn; and He could comfort them when life seemed a mess. They cried out to Him in pain, in doubt, in fear, in longing, and in lament. And each one was drawn into a deeper relationship with God as a result.

That's what I want—a deeper relationship with God through prayer. And because you've chosen to do this study, I'm guessing you do too. So let's begin!

Praying for you on bended knee,
Crickett

JESUS:
A MODEL PRAYER

Are you satisfied with your prayer life? Does time alone with God in prayer hold the highest priority in your day, or does it get pushed aside by the urgent? Are you just saying words, or are you pouring out your heart to the Father? What is most of your prayer time focused on—asking for personal needs, worshiping God, giving thanks? Prayer is more than just asking God for things; it's about the relationship.

D. Martyn Lloyd-Jones wrote, "The highest picture that you can ever have of man is to look at him on his knees waiting upon God. That is the highest achievement of man, it is his noblest activity. Man is never greater than when he is there in communion and contact with God."[1] If we believe this is true, wouldn't we spend more time on our knees in prayer?

To be honest, I would guess most of us struggle with prayer. Busyness of life often crowds out time alone with God to pray. And when we do pray, we often bring Him our grocery list of things we want as we rush out the door. For some, prayer has become nothing more than a routine ritual out of a sense of obligation. But God wants it to be about the relationship, not a ritual.

Jesus knew He needed time alone with the Father. No matter how busy He was, He always took time to get away and pray. In Luke 11:1, one of the disciples saw Jesus praying and asked Him to teach them how to pray. Jesus answered by giving them a model to follow. We often refer to this as the "Lord's Prayer." This model prayer would guide the disciples (and us) through essential components of prayer and teach us how to pray like Jesus did.

We begin this study on prayer by looking at His model for praying. Ask God to teach you fresh application about prayer. Don't just recite the words, but use them to guide you through a time of personal, powerful prayer.

"In this prayer Jesus laid down the principles governing man's relationship to God, and these are relevant to believers in every age. It should be noted that He did not say, 'Pray in these precise words,' but 'Pray, then, in this way' (v.9). He was giving a pattern, not an inflexible form. The exact words employed may vary greatly, while the individual prayer itself conforms to the pattern given."[2]

J. OSWALD SANDERS

WORSHIP

How do you begin your time of prayer? I admit I often begin prayer with my list of needs, but that's not how Jesus began His model prayer. He began with worship. When we approach God the Father in adoration and worship, it brings our worries and anxieties into perspective as we focus on God. Why wouldn't we begin with worship?

The New Testament uses the Greek words *góny* ("knee")/*gonypetéo* ("bend the knee") that give a picture of bowing the knee in prayer to God and paying homage to Jesus. Bending the knee is a physical gesture of worship that expresses "an inner attitude of adoration, respect, and humility."[3]

Let's go now on bended knee to worship Him.

Father, I turn my focus to You, my Creator, my sovereign Lord,
my faithful God who loves me unconditionally. I bow my knees to
worship You and You alone.

LOOKING TO GOD'S WORD
MATTHEW 6:9-13

1. Read the entire passage of Matthew 6:9–13. Today we will focus on verse 9. Write it below.

2. In this model, Jesus begins by focusing our attention on God in an attitude of worship: "Our Father." What does the term *Father* imply? How should we respond to God as our Father?

Sadly, not all fathers are wonderful, still what are some characteristics that we hope they have?

loving, adventurous, good will,

3. What is significant about **our** Father instead of **my** Father?

4. "Our Father who is in heaven." Why is it significant that He is in heaven?

5. "Hallowed be Your name." What does the word *hallowed* mean?

Summer series

6. What are some of God's names? (You might begin by looking at Psalm 91:1, which gives us two names.) How can we make His name hallowed in our lives?

LOOKING UPWARD

7. What is your view of God when you pray to Him? How do you think of Him?

8. How does your relationship with your earthly father affect the way you look at and approach your heavenly Father?

Does this shame God?

9. How does worshiping God impact your life?

LOOKING DEEPER

10. Read the parallel passage in Luke 11:1–4. What instructions concerning prayer does Jesus give His disciples?

11. How does this passage differ from the Matthew passage?

LOOKING REFLECTIVELY

When we worship, we turn our focus to the One we are worshiping. All other things fade into the background—our worries and cares, other people we might look to, and things we value. Worship brings us to God in a posture of adoration and humility. We acknowledge who He is, and we praise Him for His attributes. Worship prepares our hearts to be attentive to God.

Spend time worshiping your heavenly Father. "Our Father who is in heaven, hallowed be Your name." Use one or more of these suggestions to help you get started.

- Sing praises to Him. Listen to worship music.
- Praise Him as you read through a psalm or other passage focused on His attributes. (Psalm 8 is a good one to use.)
- Be quiet for a few minutes and reflect on His character.
- Write your own psalm of praise to Him.

X

We're back to Quiet Time or a Rule. Psalm 8 - 518

"And supreme among our goals in life is that we would 'hallow' that name. Glorify it. Esteem it. Draw others' attention to it. Stand amazed at it and at all it represents. . . . In placing this petition at the beginning of His model prayer, Jesus declared that no other item on our prayer list—no health concern, no relational breakdown, no financial shortfall—nothing should rank higher than this single request."[4]

NANCY DEMOSS WOLGEMUTH

WEEK 1 | DAY 2
SURRENDER

"I Surrender All" is one of my favorite hymns. Yet when I think about the words, I realize just how hard it is to surrender all to God. My tendency is to keep things under my control instead of handing everything over to Him. I often want my way instead of seeking what He wants for me. However, Jesus guides us in this prayer to ask for the Father's will and surrender our will to Him. He modeled this for us as He prayed in the Garden of Gethsemane. Are we willing to ask for God's will to be done, even if it may not be what we desire?

Lord, I surrender all to You—my desires, the work of my hands, my aspirations, my possessions, my relationships, and yes, even my life. Your will, not mine, be done.

LOOKING TO GOD'S WORD
MATTHEW 6:9-13

1. Reread the entire passage of Matthew 6:9–13. Today we will focus on verse 10. Write it below.

2. What does it mean to pray, "Your kingdom come"?

3. We are also to pray, "Your will be done." What heart attitude do we need in order to pray for God's will to be done?

4. How does praying for His will to be done relate to praying for His kingdom to come? Why does He mention His will being done on earth as it is in heaven? What does this imply?

5. What specifics of God's will do the verses below give? What verses would you add to this list concerning God's will?

1 Thessalonians 4:3
1 Thessalonians 5:16–19
1 Peter 2:13–15

LOOKING UPWARD

6. How can we know God's will?

7. Do our prayers change God's will or plan? Can they? Explain your answer.

8. If not, why do we pray?

LOOKING DEEPER

9. Jesus instructed His disciples to pray for God's will to be done. He followed this model when He prayed in the Garden of Gethsemane. Read Matthew 26:36–44. List your observations about Jesus' prayer in the Garden.

LOOKING REFLECTIVELY

In his commentary, John MacArthur explains what it means to pray, "Your kingdom come." He says, "Our greatest desire should be to see the Lord reigning as King in His kingdom, to have the honor and authority that have always been His but that He has not yet come to claim. . . . To pray *Thy kingdom come* is to pray for the program of the eternal Deity to be fulfilled, for Christ to come and reign as King of kings and Lord of lords. His program and His plan should be the preoccupation of our lives and of our prayers."[5]

- Are you praying for God's will on this earth to be done or your will?
- Are you praying for His return and waiting expectantly for His eternal Kingdom? Ask Him to show you how to spend your time for Him as you wait for His coming.
- Is Jesus Lord of your life? Have you yielded your life to His rule? If not, what area(s) are you holding onto? What are you having trouble letting go of?
- Ask Him to give you strength and grace to surrender all to Him.
- Sing and ponder the words to this hymn, "I Surrender All."[6]

All to Jesus I surrender,
All to Him I freely give;
I will ever love and trust Him,
In His presence daily live.

I surrender all,
I surrender all;
All to Thee, my blessed Savior,
I surrender all.

All to Jesus I surrender,
Humbly at His feet I bow;
Worldly pleasures all forsaken,
Take me, Jesus, take me now.

"Lord, if what I ask for does not please You, neither would it please me. My desires are put into Your hands to be corrected. Strike the pen through every petition that I offer that is not right. And put in whatever I have omitted, even though I might not have desired it had I considered it . . . 'Not as I will, but as Thou wilt.'"[7]

CHARLES SPURGEON

SUPPLICATION

Today's verse focuses on supplication, asking God for something. We rarely have trouble asking God, but are we asking for the right things and in the right way? God wants us to ask, but He also wants us to trust Him with the answers. Are we asking according to His will or our will? Jesus gave His disciples instructions on what to ask for in prayer. How well do our prayers line up with His instructions?

*Lord, teach me how to pray and ask for things according to
Your will and in a way that pleases You. Teach me how to hold things
loosely and trust You for the answers.*

LOOKING TO GOD'S WORD
MATTHEW 6:9-13

1. Reread the entire passage of Matthew 6:9–13. Today we will focus on verse 11. Write this verse below.

2. What is *our daily bread*?

3. Read Philippians 4:6. What instructions does Paul give concerning prayer? What are we to do, and what are we not to do?

11 St 4: 4 - 6   X

4. Why would giving thanks be important?

5. List your observations from Philippians 4:19. How does this verse relate to Matthew 6:11?

LOOKING UPWARD

6. If God knows what we need, why should we pray for it?

7. How do we distinguish needs from desires?

8. Some Christians believe asking for God to address physical needs shows a lack of faith. How would you respond to that?

LOOKING DEEPER

9. Read Psalm 104:10–28. How does God provide for His creation? Thank Him for His provisions and the way He provides.

LOOKING REFLECTIVELY

I have lived in times when money was tight, and I wasn't sure how I was going to make ends meet. But every time I have been in need, God provided in special ways and in His perfect timing. He has never let me go without something I truly needed. He is faithful to provide for us.

> Pray for your daily bread (your personal needs) today. Acknowledge your dependence on Him to provide. (Your needs may be more than physical needs.)

Write down ways you've seen Him provide your *daily bread* this week.

Pray for the needs of others.

Write out Philippians 4:19. Thank Him for being your provider.

"Prayer is not appointed for the furnishing of God with the knowledge of what we need, but it is designed as a confession to Him of our sense of the need. In this, as in everything, God's thoughts are not as ours. God requires that His gifts should be sought for."[8]

A. W. PINK

CONFESSION AND FORGIVENESS

Confession is vital to spiritual growth. We will continue to sin as long as we are in these earthly bodies. And when we sin, we need to confess as soon as the Holy Spirit convicts us. God has already forgiven us through Christ's death on the cross, but our confession acknowledges we are aware of our sin and we want to turn from it. As we confess, we are expressing our gratitude for His payment for all our sins. It's also important, in light of His forgiveness of us, that we forgive others. Jesus addresses forgiveness in today's lesson.

Lord, keep me sensitive to the Holy Spirit convicting me of sin.
Thank You for paying the penalty for my sins and forgiving me
once for all. Help me extend that forgiveness to others,
especially those who are difficult to forgive.

LOOKING TO GOD'S WORD
MATTHEW 6:9-13

1. Reread Matthew 6:9–13. Today we will focus on verse 12. Write it below.

2. If Jesus forgave our sins through His death on the cross, why does He tell us to ask for forgiveness? What does He mean here?

3. He continues to discuss forgiveness in verses 14–15. What does Jesus mean in verse 15 when He says, "But if you do not forgive others, then your Father will not forgive your transgressions"? Does this mean Jesus will only forgive us if we forgive others?

4. If we refuse to forgive someone, what does that reveal about our heart and attitude toward God?

LOOKING UPWARD

5. Can someone be a believer if he can't forgive others? Explain your answer.

6. How does it affect you if you continue to go for a period of time without confessing your sins?

7. How would you counsel someone who is struggling to believe God could forgive her sin?

LOOKING DEEPER

8. Jesus tells a parable in Matthew 18:21–35. List principles for forgiveness from these verses.

461

9. How does this parable relate to Matthew 6:12, 14–15?

LOOKING REFLECTIVELY

I first heard the gospel when I was a young girl. Even though I was only nine years old, I knew I was a sinner and could never be good enough to earn my salvation and forgiveness of sins on my own. Only Jesus could pay that price through His death on the cross. When I accepted Jesus as my personal Savior, I prayed to Him—thanking Him for dying on the cross for my sins and confessing my sin and inadequacy to pay the penalty myself. He forgave all my sins—past, present, and future—with His blood on the cross. He paid the penalty for me. I'm forgiven, but I still sin. And every time I sin, I need to confess to God in order to restore my fellowship with Him. My relationship with Him doesn't change when I sin—I'm still His child. However, my fellowship with Him is hindered because of unconfessed sin.

- Have you accepted Christ's death on the cross for your sins? Then you are forgiven. If you haven't, take a moment now and pray to Him, acknowledging your sin and accepting His payment for your sins on the cross. Thank Him for being your Savior and Lord.
- Do you doubt His forgiveness for something in your past? The blood of Christ covers your sins (all of them). You are forgiven.
- Keep short accounts with God. Do you need to confess anything? Agree with God it is sin. Name it, thank Him for His forgiveness on the cross, and turn away from it.
- Are you struggling with forgiving someone who has hurt or wronged you? If so, ask God to help you forgive them. The feelings may not be there at first, but by faith, forgive those people with a sincere heart. Pray for them. God will work in your heart as you are obedient to forgive.
- Meditate on Psalm 103:8–14. Write your thoughts below. What stands out to you from this psalm?

"Nothing humbles the soul like sacred and intimate communion with the Lord; yet there is a sweet joy in feeling that He knows all, and, notwithstanding, loves us still."[9]

J. HUDSON TAYLOR

PROTECTION

Every day we face spiritual battles. Some are obvious; others are subtle. We have an enemy who doesn't want us to follow God, so he tries to distract us with his fiery darts—accusations, lies, guilt, self-doubt, discouragement. As a result, we need to pray for protection in the spiritual battle around us. Jesus emphasizes this in His instructions to the disciples concerning how to pray. We'll also look at His prayer for the disciples and other believers recorded in John 17. Jesus saw the need to pray for protection for believers from the enemy, and so should we. Are you facing a spiritual battle today? Turn to Him in prayer. Don't try fighting the battle alone.

Lord, keep me from temptations. Help me look to You for strength
instead of trying to fight these spiritual battles on my own.
Protect me from the enemy. Keep me close to You.

LOOKING TO GOD'S WORD
MATTHEW 6:9–13

1. Read Matthew 6:9–13 again, even out loud. Today we will focus on verse 13. Write it below.

2. Some believe this is two petitions; others say it's one. I lean toward the view it is one petition with two parts. The first part is, "Do not lead us into temptation." What do you think Jesus means by this?

3. The second part of the petition is, "Deliver us from evil." What kind of evil is He referring to?

4. Read John 17, Jesus' High Priestly Prayer. He prayed this prayer after He washed the disciples' feet and before Judas's betrayal of Him. Jesus knew this was His last night with the disciples, and He prayed for them. We can divide this prayer into three sections, according to whom He prayed for. In each section below, write down whom He prayed for and what He prayed for them.

- 17:1–5

- 17:6–19

- 17:20–26

5. What does Jesus' prayer reveal about His heart toward the Father? Describe their relationship.

6. What does His prayer reveal about His heart toward believers?

7. In verse 17, He prays, "Sanctify them in the truth." **Sanctify** means to "set apart for special use. A believer is to be distinct from the world's sin, its values, and its goals."[10] What is the truth? How does the truth sanctify us, setting us apart from the world for God?

LOOKING UPWARD

8. What do you learn about prayer from Jesus' prayer in John 17? What stands out to you? As we look at His example, what should our prayers focus on?

9. How does God strengthen and protect us from the evil one? What verses come to mind? (One I think of is 1 John 4:4.)

LOOKING DEEPER

10. Read Ephesians 6:10–13 and describe the evil we are up against.

11. What instructions does Paul give the Ephesians in Ephesians 6:18–20 concerning prayer?

1148

X

LOOKING REFLECTIVELY

I hate to admit it, but I don't always pray for protection from the enemy. It's easy to become complacent and forget that we're in a spiritual battle. But that's exactly what Satan wants us to do. If we're not thinking about the battles around us, we won't take time to pray and put the armor of God on. Jesus guides us to pray for protection against the temptations of Satan.

- What temptations are you struggling with today? How are you handling them?

- The end of verse 13 in the NASB reads, "For Yours is the kingdom and the power and the glory forever. Amen." This is missing in early manuscripts.[11] However, it is a good reminder for us to begin and end our time in prayer with acknowledging God's sovereignty and majesty.

- Spend time today using either the Lord's Prayer in Matthew 6 or the High Priestly Prayer in John 17 to guide you through a time of prayer. Don't just repeat the words, but let them lead you as you go before the Lord in prayer.

As we end this week's lesson, take time to write out your own prayer in the space below or in your prayer journal. Following how Jesus modeled prayer in the verses we studied this week, write a prayer that focuses on worship, thanksgiving, surrender, confession, and protection. Or you may want to write a prayer on just one of these areas.

_____

_____

_____

_____

_____

_____

_____

"O Lord God, Thou are my protecting arm, fortress, refuge, shield, buckler. Fight for me and my foes must flee; uphold me and I cannot fall; Strengthen me and I stand unmoved, unmovable. Equip me and I shall receive no wound; stand by me and Satan will depart . . ."[12]

FROM *THE VALLEY OF VISION*

PAUL: A PRAYER OF INTERCESSION

When someone tells me they prayed for me, it makes me smile! When I pray for others, it draws me into their lives. We can easily pray for the specific needs of others—health, financial issues, marriage problems, a job. But how much time do we spend praying for their spiritual growth and love for God?

Paul prayed powerful prayers for the believers with whom he was involved, and he probably spent hours on his knees in prayer. He prayed with passion, with purpose, and from the heart. He wanted to see these believers grow in their faith and move forward to spiritual maturity.

We could spend an entire study just looking at the prayers of Paul, but this lesson focuses on only one of them. I encourage you to memorize it. Spend time every day this week praying it for others and for yourself. Consider Paul's words and why he prayed in this way. Paul was a prayer warrior. Imagine the impact we could make for God's kingdom if we prayed like this every day for those around us.

AN OVERVIEW OF PAUL'S PRAYER

Do you struggle with knowing how to pray for others? Paul gives us a great example to go by as he prayed for the Ephesian believers in Ephesians 3:14–21. This is one of my favorite prayers in the Bible, and I have often used it to guide me in praying for others. Today we will look at Paul's prayer in its entirety. Ask God to protect you from distractions. Be attentive to what He wants to teach you through this prayer.

> *Lord, sometimes I don't know how to pray. Teach me from*
> *Paul's prayer how to intercede for others. Keep me from just saying*
> *words. Help me pray from the heart and for those things of*
> *eternal significance.*

LOOKING TO GOD'S WORD
EPHESIANS 3:14–21

1. Begin by reading Paul's prayer in Ephesians 3:14–21. Circle any words or phrases that stand out to you. Write them down.

2. How would you describe Paul's prayer? What is the tone?

3. What are his specific requests?

4. What is Paul's desire for the Ephesian believers?

LOOKING UPWARD

5. How would you describe the tone of your prayers?

6. If others were to study a prayer you wrote, what would stand out to them? What would be the focus of your prayer?

LOOKING DEEPER

Paul prayed for all the churches he was involved with. Let's take a look at his prayer for the Colossian church and how it compares to his prayer for the Ephesians.

7. Read Paul's prayer for the Colossians in Colossians 1:9–12.

8. What does he pray for them?

9. How does it compare to his prayer for the Ephesians?

LOOKING REFLECTIVELY

Some of my most precious times in prayer have been when I've used Paul's prayers to guide me in praying for others. I actually prayed this prayer for the women in my church my first year as the Women's Ministry Director. Paul's prayers addressed spiritual needs we all have, and he demonstrated how to pray for the spiritual growth of those God has placed in our lives. His prayers also give us a glimpse into the depth of his relationship with Jesus.

Use Paul's prayer in Ephesians 3 today to pray for others and for yourself. Personalize it. Try reading it in different versions.

"The character of our praying will determine the character of our ministries. Prayer makes our words strong, gives them power, makes them stick. In every anointed ministry, prayer has always been a serious business. We must be pre-eminently people of prayer."[1]

E. M. BOUNDS

THE RELATIONSHIP
WITH GOD

What do our prayers reflect about our relationship with God and how we view Him? Do we believe God is powerful enough to do the impossible and loving enough to do what's best for us? Do we come to Him demanding our requests, or do we ask in humility? Are our prayers about getting things we want or about getting to know Him more intimately? We should begin our time in prayer by focusing on the One to whom we're praying. Paul began his prayer for the Ephesians by focusing on God the Father.

Lord, I confess I don't always begin my prayers with worship. Take away the distractions that would keep me from turning my eyes to You. Help me focus on You instead of my concerns and worries.

LOOKING TO GOD'S WORD
EPHESIANS 3:14–15

1. Paul begins his prayer with the words, "For this reason . . ." Look at the preceding context in Ephesians 1 and 2. What is the reason for Paul's prayer in light of this context?

2. Paul said, "I bow my knees . . ." in Ephesians 3:14. What does that posture suggest about his attitude toward God?

3. To whom is he praying?

4. What does he mean by the phrase, "the Father, from whom every family in heaven and on earth derives its name" (Eph. 3:14–15)? How would this encourage us?

LOOKING UPWARD

5. Does our posture in prayer matter to God—whether we sit, kneel, lay face down or face up, stand, or shut our eyes? What are your thoughts on this?

LOOKING DEEPER

6. This is not Paul's first prayer for the Ephesians. His first prayer for them is recorded in Ephesians 1:15–23. What does he pray for them in this first prayer?

7. What is his focus for them?

8. How does the prayer in Ephesians 1 compare and contrast to the one in Ephesians 3?

LOOKING REFLECTIVELY

Paul's prayers always focus on God's attributes—His love, His power, His mercy, His grace . . . Paul knows his God. When we pray, how much time do we spend focusing on God's character? To be a prayer warrior like Paul, we have to spend time praising and worshiping God, reflecting on His character.

- Begin your time of prayer today focusing on God's attributes. Which ones comfort you most and why?
- Personalize Paul's prayer in Ephesians 1:15–23. Pray through it in your own words for someone today, or write out a prayer below or in your prayer journal.

"Prayer is not getting the Lord's attention but allowing Him to lead us in praying for what He is more ready to give than we may be to ask."[2]

LLOYD JOHN OGILVIE

THE REQUESTS (PART 1)

Do we recognize we are completely helpless to do life on our own? A desperate dependence on the Lord is what makes our prayers heartfelt and honest instead of just words spoken out of obligation and guilt. When we have a felt need, we are drawn to prayer. When we feel adequate on our own to handle something, we don't sense the urgency of prayer.

We will spend the next two days looking at Paul's prayer requests for the Ephesians in Ephesians 3. He goes beyond praying for good health, safety, and material provisions. He wants them to grow in their walks with God and to draw their strength from Him. What a great example to follow as we pray for others (and ourselves).

Lord, I confess I often step out in my own strength. Keep reminding me Your strength is sufficient, not mine. I ask You to strengthen me through the power of Your Holy Spirit today.

LOOKING TO GOD'S WORD
EPHESIANS 3:14-19

1. What is the first thing Paul prays for the Ephesians in verse 16?

2. What does it mean, "according to the riches of His glory" (Eph. 3:16)?

3. What does Paul mean by the "inner man" in verse 16? (See also 2 Cor. 4:16.)

4. According to Paul's prayer, what is the source of strength?

5. Some commentators say Paul is making four requests for the Ephesians. Others say two, and some believe there is only one. How many requests do you see in Paul's prayer?

LOOKING UPWARD

6. Our strength comes from the Spirit of Christ indwelling us. How have you seen the power of the Holy Spirit at work in your life strengthening you?

LOOKING DEEPER

7. Paul begins this letter to the Ephesians in Chapter 1 by telling them the riches of God's glory they now possess as believers. Read Ephesians 1:3–14, and list the riches God gives His children.

LOOKING REFLECTIVELY

This morning, as I was writing this lesson, a situation came up that brought me to my knees in weakness. I cried out, "Lord, I can't do this! It's more than I can take, and I don't have the strength." God reminded me, "Good. You realize you can do nothing apart from Me, which is right where I want you." When I find myself at the end of my strength, I know He is the only strength I have. But why do I wait until I reach the end of myself before I recognize how much I need Him?

- Are you feeling weak or inadequate? Ask Him to show you if you are drawing from your own strength instead of His.
- Are you aware of your weakness apart from Him? Draw from the power of the Holy Spirit who indwells you.
- Pray Ephesians 3:14–16 for yourself and others. Try putting it into your own words as you pray, or write out a prayer in your journal.

*"Do not strive in your own strength; cast yourself at the feet of the Lord Jesus,
and wait upon Him in the sure confidence that He is with you, and works in you
. . . Strive in prayer; let faith fill your heart—so will you be strong in the Lord,
and in the power of His might."*[3]

ANDREW MURRAY

THE REQUESTS (PART 2)

Can you imagine what it would be like to have someone praying for you the way Paul prayed for the Ephesians? Do we pray for others in this way, or do we just send up short prayers like, "Bless them, Lord"?

Yesterday we looked at the first petition Paul made for the Ephesians—"to be strengthened with power through His Spirit in the inner man" (Eph. 3:16). Today we will look at the next part of his petitions. How can you use his example to pray for others and yourself?

Lord, I need Your strength. I acknowledge I can do nothing apart from You working in me. Teach me to pray for those things of eternal value and not just temporal needs.

LOOKING TO GOD'S WORD
EPHESIANS 3:14–21

1. Reread Ephesians 3:14–21. Today we will focus on verses 16–19.

2. In verses 16–17, Paul prays they would be strengthened with power through the Holy Spirit "so that Christ may dwell in your hearts through faith . . ." Christ is already in their hearts through faith. At the point they accepted Christ as Savior, the Spirit of Christ, the Holy Spirit, came to dwell in them. What does Paul mean when he prays that Christ may dwell in their hearts through faith?

3. What does it mean to be rooted and grounded in love (v. 17)? How do we get there?

4. How does Paul describe God's love (Eph. 3:18–19)?

5. How would you describe or define:

- the breadth of God's love?

- the length of God's love?

- the height of God's love?

- the depth of God's love?

6. What does it mean to be "filled up to all the fullness of God" (v. 19)? How does that happen in light of Ephesians 4:13?

LOOKING UPWARD

7. What can you do to understand and know the love of Christ better? What helps you?

8. Can a believer fully comprehend the love of Christ? Explain your answer.

LOOKING DEEPER

9. John talks about God's love in 1 John 4:7–14. How is His love demonstrated?

10. How is His love perfected in us (v. 12)? Write down anything else that stands out to you from this passage.

LOOKING REFLECTIVELY

I learned as a little girl that Jesus loves me. We often sang, "Jesus loves me, this I know, for the Bible tells me so."[4] Over the years, God has shown me His love in many tangible ways. But there have also been times when I have doubted His love for me because of hard circumstances or "unanswered" prayers. As I've grown in my walk with Him, He's shown me that His love never wavers or changes. He LOVES me. He loves me even when my circumstances shout otherwise. He loves me when I'm unlovable. I'm still learning the breadth, length, height, and depth of God's love.

Spend time in prayer, thanking God for specific ways He has expressed His great love to you.

- Pray for a deeper comprehension of the breadth, length, height, and depth of God's love.
- Ask Him to show you any areas that are hindering you from being filled up to all the fullness of God.

"Prayer is the open admission that without Christ we can do nothing. And prayer is the turning away from ourselves to God in the confidence that He will provide the help we need. Prayer humbles us as needy and exalts God as all-sufficient."[5]

JOHN PIPER

THE BENEDICTION

Today we look at the end of Paul's prayer for the Ephesians. Paul begins and ends his prayer focusing on the Father. When we direct our hearts toward God instead of focusing on the things we're asking for, we're saying, "God, I trust You, and I have confidence You will do what's best for me according to Your plan, not mine. You are God, and I praise You."

Lord, don't let me lose sight of You. Protect me from the storms of doubt when I find myself listening to my feelings instead of Your Word. Show me Your strength and power in my life.

LOOKING TO GOD'S WORD
EPHESIANS 3:14–21

1. Read Paul's entire prayer in Ephesians 3:14–21. Today we will focus on the benediction in verses 20–21.

2. How does Paul describe God in these verses?

3. What is the power that works within us? How do we access this power?

4. What is the ultimate result Paul wants to see?

5. As you look back over this prayer, how does Paul emphasize the Trinity (Father, Son, and Spirit)?

LOOKING UPWARD

6. If we believe God is "able to do far more abundantly beyond all that we ask or think," why don't we pray more for things that seem impossible for us?

LOOKING DEEPER

7. Benedictions are declarations of God's blessings on His children. There are a number of benedictions in the New Testament epistles similar to the one Paul wrote in Ephesians 3. As you read the ones below, write or mark your observations. What are the key points of each one? What does each benediction teach us about God and His work in us?

Romans 16:25–27

> Now to Him who is able to establish you according to my gospel and the preaching of Jesus Christ, according to the revelation of the mystery which has been kept secret for long ages past, but now is manifested, and by the Scriptures of the prophets, according to the commandment of the eternal God, has been made known to all the nations, leading to obedience of faith; to the only wise God, through Jesus Christ, be the glory forever. Amen.

1 Thessalonians 5:23

Now may the God of peace Himself sanctify you entirely; and may your spirit and soul and body be preserved complete, without blame at the coming of our Lord Jesus Christ.

2 Thessalonians 2:16–17

Now may our Lord Jesus Christ Himself and God our Father, who has loved us and given us eternal comfort and good hope by grace, comfort and strengthen your hearts in every good work and word.

2 Thessalonians 3:16

Now may the Lord of peace Himself continually grant you peace in every circumstance. The Lord be with you all!

1 Timothy 1:17

Now to the King eternal, immortal, invisible, the only God, be honor and glory forever and ever. Amen.

Hebrews 13:20–21

Now the God of peace, who brought up from the dead the great Shepherd of the sheep through the blood of the eternal covenant, even Jesus our Lord, equip you in every good thing to do His will, working in us that which is pleasing in His sight, through Jesus Christ, to whom be the glory forever and ever. Amen.

Jude 24–25

Now to Him who is able to keep you from stumbling, and to make you stand in the presence of His glory blameless with great joy, to the only God our Savior, through Jesus Christ our Lord, be glory, majesty, dominion and authority, before all time and now and forever. Amen.

LOOKING REFLECTIVELY

I enjoy reading these benedictions because they remind me of what God has done for me, as well as what He wants to do for me and in me. He is able to do far more than I ask for. This prayer of Paul's in Ephesians 3 is a great example of how to pray for others and their spiritual walk. Paul was a prayer warrior, and if we follow his model in praying for others, we too can become powerful prayer warriors.

- Do you expect God to do the impossible? If not, why?
- Are you limiting God in your prayers? If so, ask God to strengthen your faith in His ability to do "far more abundantly beyond all that we ask or think" (Eph. 3:20).
- What is one thing you will apply from today's lesson?
- In light of Ephesians 3:20–21, can you trust God's answer? Will you?
- Use the benedictions above to guide you through a time of prayer and praise today.

As we end this week's lesson, take time to write out your own prayer in the space below or in your prayer journal. Pray for someone specifically and insert their name as you pray. Write your own benediction, using the verses above to guide you.

_____

_____

_____

_____

_____

_____

_____

_____

_____

_____

_____

_____

"Before you pray, bow quietly before God, just to remember and realize who He is, how near He is, how certainly He can and will help. Just be still before Him, and allow His Holy Spirit to waken and stir in your soul the childlike disposition of absolute dependence and confident expectation."[6]

ANDREW MURRAY

JOB: A PRAYER OF DESPAIR

Most of us have gone through a time of suffering and trials, and we've asked God *why?* at some point. During those times, did God seem silent? Were you angry at God? Were you honest with Him in how you were feeling? Did you trust Him in those times even if you didn't understand why? The story of Job is a story of suffering and how he walked through it. As we begin the book of Job, we observe that his relationship with God was strong. But as he faced difficult challenges, he began to question God. Job got to the point where he wished he had never been born and asked God to take his life. But in the end, he developed a deeper trust. As a result of these hard times, he came to know God in a way he had not experienced before.

We don't have time in this lesson to look at the entire book of Job, but we'll highlight the sections that focus on some of his prayers during this time of suffering. Job found himself in the middle of one spiritual attack after another from Satan. Yet as he kept his eyes on God through prayer, he was a victorious warrior over the schemes of the devil. And we can be victorious warriors too as we turn to God in prayer in the middle of our spiritual battles.

A PRAYER OF TRUST

I want a deeper walk with God, but to be honest, I don't want to go through the suffering God uses to get me there. Yet He has given me the strength to take one day at a time when I'm in the middle of a difficult season. I can look back and see how God used hard situations to draw me into a sweeter intimacy with Him. Was it worth it? Yes, although I didn't always say that when I was in the middle of it. I felt many of the emotions Job felt and even expressed some of the same frustrations. God carried me through, and He took me to a deeper place with Him. I am grateful for those times now.

We can learn a lot about others by observing how they respond to God when life gets hard. Will they trust Him and cling to Him during those difficult times, or will they become distant and bitter toward God? Job lost almost everything dear to him, and yet he expressed trust in God even when his heart was breaking. Would we respond in the same way?

Lord, help me trust You in the good times and the hard times of life.
Teach me from Job's example how to walk through difficult times in a
way that draws me closer to You and pleases You.

LOOKING TO GOD'S WORD
JOB 1

1. Read Job 1. What do you learn about Job from verses 1–5? List your observations.

2. Describe the conversation between Satan and God in verses 6–12. How do their views of Job differ?

3. God allowed Satan to test Job. How did Satan test him in verses 13–19? What did Job lose?

4. In Job 1:20–22, we get a glimpse of Job's relationship with God. How does Job respond to this testing?

5. What does his prayer in verse 21 show about Job's heart toward God? What was his perspective at this time?

LOOKING UPWARD

6. Why do you think God allowed Satan to test Job?

7. How are we able to worship God in the middle of great loss as Job did?

LOOKING DEEPER

8. Read Job 2:1–10. There are many similarities between the situation in Job 1 and Job 2. What additional commendation for Job does God give in Job 2:3?

9. What was Satan's argument in verses 4–5?

10. What did Satan do to Job in verse 7?

11. Describe the conversation between Job and his wife in verses 9–10. What stands out to you about Job's response?

LOOKING REFLECTIVELY

To be honest, these chapters are hard to read. It's difficult to picture God allowing Satan to bring pain and suffering into Job's life. Will God allow Satan to do the same with me? How would I respond if God took away my health, everything I have, and everyone I love? I don't know, but I pray I would handle it the way Job did in these two chapters. God loves us. And even when He allows pain, He still loves us. He has a purpose for everything He allows.

- Meditate on 1 Peter 5:6–11. What do you learn about the enemy? What do you learn about God? How does this passage encourage you?
- Spend time today thanking God for everything going on in your life—good and bad. Will you trust Him even if your heart is breaking? Journal your thoughts. Be honest with God about how you're feeling. You may want to write out your prayer below.

"Trust comes from resting in God's sovereignty, secure in the knowledge that He is Lord, that He maintains the right to do whatever He desires with His children's lives."[1]

NANCY DEMOSS WOLGEMUTH

PRAYERS OF LAMENT

When we are in the middle of suffering and pain, we are stretched and experience a wide range of emotions—doubt, anger, sadness, emptiness, exhaustion, and loneliness. God doesn't want us to hold those emotions in, but to cry out to Him, expressing our complaint and feelings.

Today we're going to look at two of Job's laments as he cried out to God, and from Job's example, we'll learn how to pray when life hurts. David also wrote many lament psalms as he expressed his feelings to God. Laments are a way of pouring out our hearts to Him while also expressing our trust in Him. Laments can be very powerful prayers when we combine those two things.

> *Lord, when life gets hard, I need to be honest with You about my feelings. You know what I'm feeling, but it helps to express those feelings to You. Teach me how to pray from Job's example of pouring out his heart to You in the middle of great pain.*

LOOKING TO GOD'S WORD
JOB 3:1-26

1. Read Job's lament in Job 3. How would you describe what he's feeling?

2. What is his complaint to God?

3. List his questions in verses 11–12, 20–23 that begin with "why."

4. How does he summarize what he's feeling in verses 24–26?

5. In chapters 4–5, Job's friends attempt to give him advice, but they are of no help and only make things worse. Job continues to pour out his feelings to God in chapter 7. What questions does he ask God in verses 17–21?

6. What does Job think may be the cause of his pain and suffering (v. 20)?

LOOKING UPWARD

7. How would you describe your conversations with God when you're in a difficult and painful season of life? What questions do you ask?

8. How would you encourage someone going through suffering and pain? How would you answer when they ask why they are suffering?

LOOKING DEEPER

9. In Job 7:20, Job asked God if he had sinned, implying he thought sin had brought on his suffering. How did Jesus address this in John 9:1–5?

10. What was the purpose of the man's blindness?

11. How can we apply this to our suffering today?

LOOKING REFLECTIVELY

I remember my final year at Dallas Theological Seminary. Graduation was just a few months away, and I was looking for a job in ministry, preferably in Dallas. Job interviews went well, but with each one came a closed door. I began to question what God was doing. He seemed silent and uninvolved in my life. But God was at work during that time—preparing me and preparing the job He was developing for me in Memphis. I have learned that His silence doesn't mean He's not at work. It's a time for us to trust Him while He's working.

- Perhaps you're in a season when God is silent, and it seems as if He isn't listening. Rest assured He is there and is aware of what is going on. He is sovereign and at work in ways we can't see or understand now. Don't despair, but continue to pour out your heart before Him.
- Do you have some "why" questions for God today? Write them down. Then write below them: "Even though I don't understand, I choose to trust You, Lord."
- Spend some time praying, using Psalm 13 to guide you. Write out Psalm 13:5–6.

"We may experience times of unusual closeness, when every prayer is answered in an obvious way and God seems intimate and caring. And we may also experience 'fog times,' when God stays silent, when nothing works according to formula and all the Bible promises seem glaringly false. Fidelity involves learning to trust that, out beyond the perimeter of the fog, God still reigns and has not abandoned us, no matter how it appears." [2]

PHILIP YANCEY

SEEKING ANSWERS

I have been in difficult seasons of life when I cried out to God for answers. "God, why are You allowing this to happen? Why did You say no to my prayers? How long is this going to last?" If we only knew why things were happening, we believe those answers would give us strength to go on. If we could just understand why, then we could trust God. But God never tells us we need to understand; He tells us to trust Him. He will show us answers in His timing.

Father, help me trust You when I find myself in those
dark times when You seem far away and silent. Remind me of Your
character as I turn to Your Word. Teach me patience to wait on
You when I want answers now. Thank You that You are a loving
Father, even in difficult seasons.

LOOKING TO GOD'S WORD
JOB 10

1. Read Job 10. This chapter is another prayer, a cry to God for answers. How would you describe Job's thoughts and feelings toward God and his overall perspective of life?

2. What are the questions he asks God (vv. 3–6, 8–11, 18, 20)?

In chapters 12–14, Job debated with his friends about their view of God. He also questioned God. Job knew his suffering wasn't the result of sin, but he didn't know why God was dealing with him in this way. The only explanation he could think of was that God wasn't just.[3]

3. What is Job's attitude in Job 13:13–16?

4. Verse 20 in the English Standard Version (ESV) reads, "Only grant me two things, then I will not hide myself from your face." What two things is he asking for in verse 21?

5. What else is Job asking for in Job 13:22–24?

6. God was silent to Job's requests and did not give him an answer, and Job once again settled into despair in chapter 14. Job's friends were of no help or encouragement to him. He was at a low, questioning God and feeling misunderstood by his friends. But he makes a powerful statement in Job 19:25–27. Read those verses out loud. What is the point Job is making here?

LOOKING UPWARD

7. Have you cried out to God in pain only to feel God was silent? What was the situation? How did it affect your perspective of God? Did it draw you into a deeper intimacy with Him, or did you pull back in anger, hurt, and frustration?

8. Did you later see how God's hand was at work? If so, how?

LOOKING DEEPER

9. As you walk through difficult seasons of life, how would Paul's words in Romans 8:28, 31–39 encourage you?

LOOKING REFLECTIVELY

There have been times I longed for an answer from God, even demanded an answer. Yet He was silent. Why? Because God was working in my life, teaching me to wait on Him, teaching me to trust His hand even though I didn't understand what He was doing or why. For some of those situations, I have been able to look back and see what God was doing and how He had worked for my good and His glory.

But in other situations, I may have to wait until heaven to fully understand why. God's silence doesn't mean He has turned away from us or forgotten us or become distracted by more important issues. He has never lost sight of what is happening in our lives. He is very much at work.

- Are you going through a hard season now? Are you questioning why God has allowed it or why He isn't doing something about it? Do you feel He is being silent? Do you doubt His love for you? Pour out your complaint to God as He knows how you feel. But also revere Him as the sovereign God who knows what He is doing.
- Use Psalm 62 to guide you through a time of prayer. Write down your thoughts below or in your prayer journal.

"Pouring out my heartache to God has brought me into His comforting embrace in a way I could never have imagined."[4]

CAROL KENT

GOD'S RESPONSE

Up to this point, we've been looking at Job's prayers to God. Now let's turn our attention to how God responds to Job. When we find ourselves in difficult times, we want to hear from God. We want answers. God's Word gives us assurance of His character—His love, mercy, grace, sovereignty, faithfulness, and all His attributes. Let God speak to you through His Word when you're struggling with understanding why.

> *Father, life gets hard at times, and I struggle to keep my eyes on You.*
> *I get discouraged and sometimes doubt Your love for me. Yet I know*
> *You love me, and You have a reason for everything You allow into*
> *my life. Hold me close during these challenging times. Remind me of*
> *Your truths when my heart begins to doubt.*

LOOKING TO GOD'S WORD
JOB 38

1. Job has voiced his feelings to his friends and to God. Now God speaks to Job. What was the setting from which God spoke to Job in 38:1?

2. How would you describe God's response to Job in 38:2–3?

3. Read all of Job 38. (Job 39 continues this thought.) What is the point God is making to Job?

4. Which attributes of God are emphasized in this chapter?

5. Notice how God uses questions to answer Job. Why would that be effective in this situation?

LOOKING UPWARD

6. If God were saying these words to you, how would you feel? What would you do?

7. When we blame and find fault with God, what does that reveal about our perspective of Him?

LOOKING DEEPER

8. In Job 40:1–5, God confronts Job with a piercing question and challenge. What are your observations from verses 1–2?

9. How did Job respond to God?

10. How would you describe Job's heart at this time?

LOOKING REFLECTIVELY

God's hand is in every detail of what is happening in and around our lives, even though we may not understand what He's doing at the time. We can only see a small piece of the story, but God sees the big picture. He knows exactly what He's doing to accomplish His ultimate purpose. Reading these chapters should move us to worship our Creator, our Lord, our God.

- Are you blaming God for something today? Are you questioning how He is working in you and around you? Humble yourself before Him and acknowledge His power, sovereignty, and majesty.
- Take time to worship God. Write down verses that encourage you about God's character in hard times. (Some of my favorites are Lamentations 3:22–23 and Isaiah 26:3–4.)

- Thank Him that He "causes all things to work together for good to those who love God, to those who are called according to His purpose" (Rom. 8:28).

"In praying, we are often occupied with ourselves, with our own needs, and our own efforts in the presentation of them. In waiting upon God, the first thought is of the God upon whom we wait. . . . God longs to reveal Himself, to fill us with Himself. Waiting on God gives Him time in His own way and divine power to come to us."[5]

ANDREW MURRAY

A PRAYER OF REPENTANCE

This was a hard season for Job. He suffered physical pain and loss to the point he wished he had never been born. He struggled with the questions you and I do. *Why? How long? Where are You, God? What have I done to deserve this?*

Most of the book of Job is filled with his laments—prayers pouring out his complaint to God. But when it seems as if Job will lose all hope in God, he sees Him in a fresh light, and he recognizes how God has worked in him through the pain and suffering.

> *Father, You know why I'm going through difficult things. Help me trust You even when I don't understand why. Help me focus on Your character as I walk through those times. Draw me into a closer walk with You as a result. Thank You that even when it seems You're silent, You are very much at work in ways I can't see.*

LOOKING TO GOD'S WORD
JOB 42

1. Welcome to Job 42, a turning point for Job in this journey. Read Job 42:1–6. Describe Job's heart and attitude.

2. What is Job acknowledging in verses 2–3?

3. How do Job's words in verses 4–6 indicate a change in his heart? How has Job's relationship with God changed?

4. Read Job 42:7–9. Why was God displeased with Job's friends, and what did He ask them to do?

5. Job prayed for his friends, and God accepted his prayer. Why do you think God had Job pray for them? What do you think he prayed for them?

LOOKING UPWARD

6. How has God deepened your relationship with Him through pain and suffering?

7. How have your prayers changed as a result?

LOOKING DEEPER

8. Read Job 42:10–17. How did God bless Job after he prayed for his friends?

9. Why do you think God waited until after Job prayed for his friends to bless him?

LOOKING REFLECTIVELY

It's hard to see the positives when we're in the middle of pain. I know in the final years of my mom's life, I hit low points. I didn't think I could make it much longer in caregiving and watching Mom's life dwindle to a bare existence. I questioned God. My anger exploded at times. *God, why won't You take Mom home and relieve her of her physical pain and misery?* But after it was over, I could honestly look back and see how God used that time to draw me into a sweet intimacy with Him I had not known before. He used pain for good.

- Think of a difficult time God used to deepen your walk with Him. How did you grow in your relationship with Him during that time?
- What can you do to strengthen your trust in God in a difficult season?
- How can you come alongside and encourage others going through a difficult time?

As we close this week of studying Job's prayers, take time to reflect on his prayers. Use Psalm 66 to guide you through a time of prayer, writing out your prayer below or in your prayer journal.

_____

_____

_____

_____

_____

_____

_____

_____

_____

_____

_____

_____

_____

_____

"The period of waiting for the granting of some request is often rewarded by a far greater gift than what we asked for. The Lord Himself."[6]

LLOYD JOHN OGILVIE

HANNAH: A PRAYER OF LONGING

Have you prayed fervently for something you wanted with all your heart? Perhaps it was for a specific job, a husband, a child, or a good health report. Sometimes we see God answer in the way we desire. Other times He answers in a way we had not expected and not in line with what we were hoping for. Regardless of how He answers, He loves us and has a purpose for how He answers our prayers.

This week we will study a prayer of Hannah when she was grieving over a difficult situation in her life. She went before the Lord and poured out her heart to Him, pleading for her heart's longing. And God answered with a *yes*. But sometimes we ask God for something, and He says *no* or *not yet*. Can we trust God knows what's best for us?

THE SETTING

As 1 Samuel begins, Israel is at a low point spiritually. The priesthood was corrupt, idolatry was being practiced, and the judges were dishonest. In this setting, Hannah prayed for a son. God answered and gave her Samuel, who would become instrumental in reversing those conditions. Before we get started on this week's lesson, pray this prayer with me.

> *Father, I have cried out to You for things I wanted with all my heart.*
> *Sometimes You said yes; but other times the answer was no.*
> *Help me trust You when Your answer isn't what I was hoping for.*
> *Help me rest in Your sovereign plan for my life.*

LOOKING TO GOD'S WORD
1 SAMUEL 1:1–10

1. Read 1 Samuel 1:1–10. What is Hannah's situation in verse 2?

2. Describe the relationship between Hannah and her husband, Elkanah.

3. What are the four questions Elkanah asked Hannah in verse 8?

4. Describe the relationship between Hannah and Peninnah (vv. 4–7).

5. What was the cause of Hannah's barrenness (v. 5)?

6. How did this situation impact Hannah's life? Describe her emotional, physical, and mental state. What was her focus?

LOOKING UPWARD

7. Hannah was so overwhelmed by the desire for a child she couldn't see the blessing God had given her in a husband who deeply loved her. Can you think of a situation in your life when you missed seeing God's goodness because you were so consumed by something you didn't have but desperately wanted? Describe that time—emotionally, as well as spiritually.

8. Is there someone in your life who provokes and irritates you? Or someone in the past? How did you respond?

9. What has God taught you through the situation?

LOOKING DEEPER

Elkanah had two wives. Hannah was most likely his first wife.[1] Often in those days (though it was never sanctioned by God), a man whose wife was infertile would take a second wife by whom he could bear children. Elkanah probably married Peninnah because Hannah was barren.

10. What was the situation for multiple wives in these passages?

- Genesis 16:1–3

- Genesis 30:1–4

- Genesis 30:9–10

- Deuteronomy 25:5–6

LOOKING REFLECTIVELY

All of us have desires of the heart that we long for. For some, the desire of your heart is marriage: "Lord, I long to be married." For some of you it may be just the opposite: "Lord, I wish I weren't married. Get me out of this." For others, you desire to have a child or a grandchild or to have that certain job or position. Maybe you long to have more money, to accomplish some great achievement, to be healed, or to be free of pain.

- What is your heartfelt desire today, and how is it affecting you?
- How have you seen God protect you from something not best for you by saying no to your longing?
- Are you longing for something today you don't have? Take that longing to the Lord in prayer.
- Will you trust Him to give you what's best?

Write out Psalm 37:4–5 below. What are we to do? What will God do? Meditate on these verses.

"We've seen from God's Word how even the giants of the faith struggled with their emotions. How good it is of God to let us see beyond the surface. . . . These folks were just like us. They suffered the hardships, difficulties, and tragedies of life in a fallen world. They struggled, they failed, they cried out to God, sometimes in confusion and doubt, always for help. And God came through for them. He . . . used them to have an eternal impact on their contemporaries as well as on God's people throughout the many centuries since." [2]

VICKIE KRAFT

A PRAYER FROM THE HEART

Hannah was in a difficult situation—a polygamous marriage and barrenness. She also had to deal with the other wife (with children) who provoked her. In her distress, she went to the temple and poured out her heart to God. Hannah was in a hard place, but God uses hard places to draw us into a deeper relationship with Him. He wants us to come to Him with our discouragement, bitterness, and hurts. He already knows what we're thinking, but it helps us work through the pain and the process when we verbalize to Him what we're feeling.

Lord, thank You for the hard times, even though I don't always
understand why You've placed me in them. Help me remember
You are working in ways I can't see. Strengthen me to
walk by faith and trust You.

LOOKING TO GOD'S WORD
1 SAMUEL 1:10–18

1. Read 1 Samuel 1:10–18. What observations do you make about Hannah's prayer?

2. In verse 11, we see Hannah beginning with worship even in the midst of her pain. She addresses God as "O Lord of hosts." Why might she have used this title for God in her prayer? Which attribute(s) is that name referring to?

3. What is her request?

4. What vow does she make to God?

5. Why did Eli think she was drunk?

6. How does she respond to Eli?

7. How would you describe Hannah?

8. What term did she repeatedly use for herself? What does that indicate about her relationship with God?

LOOKING UPWARD

9. Notice in verse 18 that when Hannah left, she ate and "her face was no longer sad." God had not answered her prayer yet, so why do you think her countenance changed?

10. Some have said Hannah was bargaining with God. Was she? Should we pray in this manner? Why or why not?

LOOKING DEEPER

11. Hannah promised God she would devote the boy to His service as a Nazirite. What do you learn about being a Nazirite from Numbers 6:1–8?

LOOKING REFLECTIVELY

Having children was a sign of God's blessing. The Israelites considered the inability to bear children as a curse because the family name could not be carried on without a son. A woman's duty in that culture was to bear children, especially sons, and her self-worth was tied up in that. Hannah was probably dealing with her sense of self-worth and may have felt like a failure because she was not able to live up to the cultural expectation of bearing children. To make things worse, she had the other wife provoking her and irritating her.

Hannah took her bitterness and distress to the Lord in prayer and reordered her priorities. She no longer wanted a child just for herself, but she committed to dedicate the son she prayed for to the Lord.

- Is there something you long for that God has not given you? How are you handling it?
- Why do you long for it?
- If God says *no* to your request, can you trust His sovereign hand in your life and rest in the truth that He loves you and wants to give what's best for you?
- Spend time today in prayer with the Lord. Pour out your heart to Him. Be honest about your longings. Journal your prayer. Ask Him to show you any wrong motives in your requests. Give Him the longings of your heart and trust Him to answer as He deems best.

"That she would offer her son to God's service for life was similar to asking that God would lead your child into 'the ministry.' Asking that he would be a lifetime Nazirite was similar to asking that your child would dedicate himself completely to God, not just by profession but also by conviction. Hannah showed that she desired the honor of Yahweh more than simply gaining relief from her abusers. She wanted to make a positive contribution to God's program for Israel by providing a godly leader, not just to bear a child."[3]

THOMAS CONSTABLE

THE ANSWER

God heard Hannah's prayer, and He answered by giving her the precious child she had asked for. Would she be faithful to her promise and give her son back to God when it was time? It would have been tempting for Hannah to rationalize her way out of keeping her vow. Elkanah could have annulled it according to Numbers 30, but he supported his wife and the promise she had made to God. They both knew the priority of obedience to God.

> *Father, thank You for Your answers to prayer, even when*
> *it's not a yes. I'm learning how to thank You and trust You when*
> *Your answer is no, but I still have a long way to go. Help me rest*
> *in Your sovereign plan for my life.*

LOOKING TO GOD'S WORD
1 SAMUEL 1:19–28

1. In verse 19, God remembered Hannah. What does that mean? How did God answer her prayer (v. 20)?

2. Scripture records nothing about Hannah's thoughts or emotions during the time after Samuel was born. What do you observe about Hannah from this passage?

3. What do you learn about her relationship with God?

4. What do you think Elkanah meant in verse 23 when he said, "only may the LORD confirm His word"?

5. Scripture doesn't tell us what age Samuel was when Hannah took him to Shiloh. But it is believed that most Hebrew women nursed their children to around the age of three. Why would this be a good age to take Samuel to Eli?

6. What observations do you make about Elkanah in this passage?

LOOKING UPWARD

7. How do you respond when God doesn't answer your prayer in the way you'd like? What has helped you trust Him with the answers?

LOOKING DEEPER

8. What do these passages say about the serious nature of vows?

- Numbers 30

- Deuteronomy 23:21–23

LOOKING REFLECTIVELY

God answered Hannah's prayer for a son in His timing. Hannah may have been praying for a child for years. Why did God answer then and not sooner? God's purpose and timing are perfect. Samuel would grow up to be a judge, a prophet, and a spiritual leader to a nation in need of spiritual leadership. He would also play a part in designating the first two kings of Israel—Saul and David.

- Are you praying for your children, grandchildren, nieces, and nephews to be used by the Lord? Pray for them now.
- Are you willing to dedicate your children to the Lord, even if that means they may end up serving Him in a far-away land? Write out that prayer now.

I remember when I first called my mom to tell her I was moving to East Asia for missionary work. God had clearly led me, and I knew this was His path for me. But it was difficult for Mom to hear. She actually hung up on me because she couldn't talk about it. I called her back later and explained how God had led me. I didn't want to say no to the Lord. She eventually realized she had to let go of me and allow me to follow His calling. My mother became my strongest supporter and prayer warrior. Was it easy for her to see me go to the other side of the world for four years? No. There were many tears. But I am grateful that Mom entrusted me to the Lord's hands as I sought to serve Him wholeheartedly.

- Spend time with the Lord, presenting your life as an offering to Him. Hold your children and family in an open hand, willing to let God do as He pleases with them.

"The things that He puts into our hands are possibly put there that we may have the opportunity of showing what is in our heart. Oh, that there were in us a fervor of love that would lead us to examine everything that belongs to us, to ascertain how it might be made a means of showing our affection to Christ!"[4]

GEORGE BOWEN

A PRAYER OF THANKSGIVING

When the time came for Hannah to give her son to God, she stayed true to her vow. She and Elkanah left Samuel with Eli at the tabernacle to serve the Lord the rest of his life. Her circumstances were hard—saying goodbye to the young child she had so fervently asked God for. Her prayer of thanksgiving in 1 Samuel 2 shows her deep awareness of who God is, her confidence in His sovereignty, and her source of joy in the midst of letting go of a priceless possession, her child.

Father, thank You for all You do for me. Give me a heart
of gratitude, and keep me from taking Your goodness for granted.
Help me keep all Your gifts in an open hand, ready to give
them back to You if and when You ask.

LOOKING TO GOD'S WORD
1 SAMUEL 2:1–10

1. As you read Hannah's prayer of thanksgiving in 1 Samuel 2:1–10, what is the source of her joy and thanksgiving? In whom is she rejoicing?

2. In verse 1, she refers to her "heart," her "horn," and her "mouth." What does she say about each?

3. **"Horn** symbolizes God's strength and dignity."[5] What does she mean by the phrase, "my horn is exalted in the LORD"?

4. What is the main theme of her prayer?

5. On which attributes of God does Hannah focus?

6. List all God does in this passage. Note the contrasts Hannah makes in her prayer.

7. This song of thanksgiving is also Messianic. How do we see this in verse 10?

LOOKING UPWARD

8. Hannah refers to God as a "rock" in verse 2. What does a rock signify? How is God a "rock" in your life?

9. What personal application can you make from this song of thanksgiving?

LOOKING DEEPER

Hannah's song of thanksgiving in 1 Samuel 2 was used twice in biblical poetry. It served as the basis for Psalm 113, and both songs were used and developed further in Mary's Magnificat, which we will look at tomorrow. Read Psalm 113.

10. How is it similar to Hannah's song of praise?

LOOKING REFLECTIVELY

When we see God answer our prayers in the way we desire, our hearts are full of praise. Every time I raise support for a mission trip and ask God to provide, there's always that little twinge of doubt—will the money come in? Yet every time, God faithfully provides. Seeing God's mighty hand at work sends me to my knees in worship and praise of His goodness and love and power to do what seems impossible for me.

- How have you seen answers to your prayers recently?
- Praise Him for His attributes mentioned in both songs of praise.
- Use Psalm 113 to guide you through a time of praise, worship, and prayer before the Lord. Feel free to write out a prayer following the same pattern of this psalm.

"What great things she (Hannah) says of God. She takes little notice of the particular mercy she was now rejoicing in, does not commend Samuel for the prettiest child, the most toward and sensible for his age that she ever saw, as fond parents are too apt to do. No, she overlooks the gift and praises the giver; whereas most forget the giver and fasten only on the gift. Every stream should lead us to the fountain; and the favours we receive from God should raise our admiration of the infinite perfections there are in God."[6]

MATTHEW HENRY

MARY'S MAGNIFICAT

How often do we stop and sing praises to God when we've seen Him answer prayer in the way we had hoped? Hannah wrote her beautiful song of thanksgiving to God after He gave her Samuel. Today we will look at another mother's song of thanksgiving—Mary, mother of Jesus. She had not asked God for a son, but she realized the great gift this promised Son, Jesus, was going to be to the world. Both Hannah and Mary sang hymns of praise. Mary incorporated some of Hannah's song into her own "Magnificat." If you were to write a song of praise to God, what would it say? Which attributes would you praise God for?

Father, thank You for loving me enough to send Your only Son for me. Thank You for this sacrifice. I want to honor You with my life and sing praises to You for all You have done.

LOOKING TO GOD'S WORD
LUKE 1:39–55

1. Read Luke 1:39–45 to determine the setting. Describe the situation.

2. Read Luke 1:46–55, Mary's "Magnificat." How does Mary view God?

3. What does she praise Him for?

4. What do Hannah and Mary have in common?

5. How do Mary's words compare to Hannah's? For your convenience, I have included the two texts below. What observations do you make as you compare these two songs of praise to God? As things stand out to you, circle them or write your thoughts in the space provided.

1 Samuel 2:1–10 (ESV)

And Hannah prayed and said, "My heart exults in the LORD; my horn is exalted in the LORD. My mouth derides my enemies, because I rejoice in your salvation. There is none holy like the LORD: for there is none besides you; there is no rock like our God. Talk no more so very proudly, let not arrogance come from your mouth; for the LORD is a God of knowledge, and by him actions are weighed. The bows of the mighty are broken, but the feeble bind on strength. Those who were full have hired themselves out for bread, but those who were hungry have ceased to hunger. The barren has borne seven, but she who has many children is forlorn. The LORD kills and brings to life; he brings down to Sheol and raises up. The LORD makes poor and makes rich; he brings low and he exalts. He raises up the poor from the dust; he lifts the needy from the ash heap to make them sit with princes and inherit a seat of honor. For the pillars of the earth are the LORD's, and on them he has set the world. He will guard the feet of his faithful ones, but the wicked shall be cut off in darkness, for not by might shall a man prevail. The adversaries of the LORD shall be broken to pieces; against them he will thunder in heaven. The LORD will judge the ends of the earth; he will give strength to his king and exalt the horn of his anointed."

Luke 1:46–55 (ESV)

And Mary said, "My soul magnifies the Lord, and my spirit rejoices in God my Savior, for he has looked on the humble estate of his servant. For behold, from now on all generations will call me blessed; for he who is mighty has done great things for me, and holy is his name. And his mercy is for those who fear him from generation to generation. He has shown strength with his arm; he has scattered the proud in the thoughts of their hearts; he has brought down the mighty from their thrones and exalted those of humble estate; he has filled the hungry with good things, and the rich he has sent away empty. He has helped his servant Israel, in remembrance of his mercy, as he spoke to our fathers, to Abraham and to his offspring forever."

LOOKING UPWARD

6. Both Hannah and Mary were able to praise God for His answers to prayer. How was Hannah able to offer praise after giving up her beloved son for whom she had prayed? How are we able to offer praise when we have to let go of something or someone we cherish?

LOOKING DEEPER

7. Read these two prayers of praise again. Mark each attribute of God they mention or refer to.

LOOKING REFLECTIVELY

Hannah endured deep distress at the hand of her provoker, and she grieved because she longed for a child. She poured out her heart to the One who can do all things. Her prayer characterizes a wholehearted devotion to God, demonstrated by her willingness to give her child back to the Lord for His glory. May we pray with the fervency and devotion seen in Hannah's prayer.

God answered Hannah's prayer with a *yes*. But sometimes He answers our prayers with a *no*. For years, I longed for a husband and prayed to God every day about it. I felt I could better serve God as a husband/wife team instead of as a single woman, especially on the mission field. Yet year after year, God said *no*. Finally, God brought me to the place where I realized He wants my total, undivided devotion, and He can use me more effectively as a single in ministry. He changed the longing of my heart—I no longer pray for a husband. I pray I would be wholeheartedly devoted to Him and serve Him well in my singleness.

- Spend time today being honest with God about your desires and longings. What is something you long for but God has not yet said *yes* to? Will you trust Him with the *no*?
- How have you seen Him work in your life?
- Write your own hymn of praise to God below or in your prayer journal.

_____

_____

_____

_____

_____

_____

_____

_____

_____

"What you need to do . . . is to put your will over completely into the hands of your Lord, surrendering to Him the entire control of it. Say, 'Yes, Lord, Yes!' to everything, and trust Him so to work in you to will, as to bring your whole wishes and affections into conformity with His own sweet, and lovable, and most lovely will. . . . It is wonderful what miracles God works in wills that are utterly surrendered to Him."[7]

HANNAH WHITALL SMITH

DAVID: A PRAYER OF LAMENT

When I think of David, I think of a shepherd, a young boy who defeated a giant with a slingshot and stones, a king, a man with many enemies, and most of all, a prayer warrior. The book of Psalms records many of David's prayers—prayers for protection, guidance, and strength, and prayers of thanksgiving, praise, and lament (a way of pouring out your complaint to the Lord).

In fact, sixty-seven of the psalms are considered laments. "Laments can have seven parts, including: an address to God, a review of God's faithfulness in the past, a complaint, a confession of sin or claim of innocence, a request for help, God's response, and a vow to praise God or a statement of trust in God. . . .You may not see all seven parts in each one, but the essential, ever-present part is the complaint."[1]

We looked at Job's life a few weeks ago as he poured out his heart to God in prayers of lament. Sometimes we're going to have days when our circumstances overwhelm us, people make life difficult for us, or we need direction in life. David felt all these things, and he responded by pouring out his heart to God. He was honest about his feelings, but he always ended his prayer with an expression of trust.

Psalm 25 is a prayer of lament written by David. As you study Psalm 25 this week, ask God to teach you how to lament.

I LIFT UP MY SOUL

Some days I unload on God, telling Him everything I'm feeling. Tears may accompany my words as I express my discouragement. But when I'm finished, I feel like a load has been lifted. David begins Psalm 25 by pouring out his heart to God, while also acknowledging his trust in God. Perhaps you need to pour out your heart to God today.

> *Father, I have hurts; some I'm very much aware of, and some*
> *I'm not. Show me what's in my heart, and help me pour out*
> *those emotions to You while acknowledging my love and trust in You.*
> *I need You. Make me attentive to Your Word and help me*
> *respond in a way that pleases You.*

LOOKING TO GOD'S WORD
PSALM 25

1. Begin by reading Psalm 25 in its entirety. How would you outline this psalm?

2. Describe David's relationship with God in this prayer.

3. Today we are going to focus on the first three verses. Read Psalm 25:1–3 again. How does David address God?

4. What does it mean to "lift up my soul" (v. 1)? How do we do that? (You might also look at other translations to see how this phrase is worded.)

5. What are David's requests in verse 2?

6. David repeats the word "ashamed" three times in verses 2–3. Repetition is used for emphasis. Why do you think he is emphasizing this word in his prayer?

7. What contrast does he make in verse 3?

LOOKING UPWARD

8. David prayed that his enemies would not exult over him. What or who are your enemies? How can you protect yourself from them?

LOOKING DEEPER

9. Read Psalm 142, another lament psalm written by David when he was hiding in a cave, presumably from Saul.

10. What was David feeling?

11. What did he ask of God?

12. How did he express his trust in God?

LOOKING REFLECTIVELY

David begins his prayer in Psalm 25 by acknowledging his trust in God. Is there an area in your life where you are struggling to trust God? If so, begin your time of prayer by being honest with God about your feelings and struggles.

Lift up your soul to the One you can trust. Write out Isaiah 26:3–4 below.

Meditate on these words. How do they encourage you today? In light of these verses, spend some time worshiping God in prayer.

"Blessed Lord, let me climb up near to thee, and love, and long, and plead, and wrestle with thee, and pant for deliverance from the body of sin, for my heart is wandering and lifeless, and my soul mourns to think it should ever lose sight of its Beloved. Wrap my life in divine love, and keep me ever desiring thee, always humble and resigned to thy will, more fixed on thyself, that I may be more fitted for doing and suffering."[2]

FROM *THE VALLEY OF VISION*

MAKE ME KNOW YOUR WAYS

Trust is vital in any relationship, but especially in our relationship with God. If we don't trust God, it will be hard to pour out our hearts to Him. God is trustworthy, even when things don't seem to make sense and we don't understand. We saw yesterday how David trusted God even though he was in a hard place. Today we see David's teachable heart as he continues to cry out to God. Pray this prayer with me before we look at David's prayer.

> *Lord, I want to trust You, but I confess there are times I get discouraged when circumstances aren't going the way I want. I know You are trustworthy. Help me focus on the truth of Your Word instead of my feelings. Give me a teachable heart, that I might learn from You. I want to know Your ways. Give me a listening, attentive heart.*

LOOKING TO GOD'S WORD
PSALM 25:4–7

1. Read Psalm 25:4–7. Which attributes of God does David focus on in these verses?

2. What contrasts does he make in verses 6–7 with the word "remember"?

3. What does David ask for?

4. What do you think David means by the phrase, "remember me" (v. 7)?

5. How do you see a teachable heart in David in these verses?

LOOKING UPWARD

6. David asks for God's guidance. How do we find God's guidance?

7. David says in verse 5, "For You I wait all the day." How do we learn to wait on God? What helps us wait?

LOOKING DEEPER

8. Read Psalm 143, another lament psalm and prayer of David for deliverance and guidance.   X

9. What was David feeling when he wrote this psalm? What was his complaint?

10. How do you see a teachable heart in David in this psalm?   X

LOOKING REFLECTIVELY

When I look for someone to disciple, one of the first things I look for is a teachable heart. In the same way, I believe God also wants us to have teachable hearts to Him. At times, I have chosen to disciple someone who wasn't teachable, and it was a struggle. It's hard to help someone grow who doesn't see their need for spiritual growth. A teachable heart speaks volumes about a person's spiritual maturity and desire to grow in their faith. Do we come to God with a teachable heart?

- What characteristics would demonstrate a teachable heart in someone? Are those characteristics present in your life? If not, what needs to change?

- Do you have trouble waiting on God? If so, what makes it hard for you? What are some results of not waiting on God?

- Use David's words in Psalm 25:4–7 to guide you through a time of prayer today. You may want to write your prayer below or in your prayer journal. Ask God to make you teachable and willing to wait on Him.

"That which I know not teach Thou me. Who, blessed Lord, teacheth like Thee? Lead my desires that they may be according to Thy will."[3]

AMY CARMICHAEL

PARDON MY SIN

As much as I hate to admit it, I sin. Every day I commit sins—negative thoughts, hurtful words, jealousy, envy, comparison, anger, pride. The list goes on. We will struggle with sin until the day He takes us to be with Him face to face. Thankfully, God has forgiven our sins because of Christ's blood on the cross, but we still need to confess our sins to Him as we commit them. Confession restores our fellowship with God as we admit our sin and express our desire to turn away from it. David was aware of his sin in Psalm 25, and he asked God to pardon his sin. May we pray in the same way.

*Father, thank You for forgiving me through Christ's death
on the cross for me. Keep me sensitive to the sins in my life.
Bring them to light through the Holy Spirit convicting me, and help
me be attentive to that conviction. Cleanse my heart, Lord.
I want to walk with You, not continue in sin.*

LOOKING TO GOD'S WORD
PSALM 25:8–11

1. How does David describe God in this passage?

2. List the three parallel statements in verses 8–9, beginning with the word "He" (directly stated or implied).

3. What are God's actions (the three verbs) in these three statements?

4. Who are the recipients of each action?

5. Why would David use the term "the humble" instead of "everyone" in verse 9?

6. What is the one request David makes of God in this section?

7. What is the connection between this request in verse 11 and the previous three verses in this section?

LOOKING UPWARD

8. What difference does it make to know all God's paths are lovingkindness and truth?

LOOKING DEEPER

9. Read Psalm 130, a Song of Ascents sung by the Jews traveling on the uphill road to Jerusalem to attend one of the three main Jewish festivals. What does the psalmist ask of God in verse 2?

10. What does he say about sin and forgiveness?

11. How does the psalmist express his trust in God? How does he view God?

12. Write down anything else that stands out to you from this psalm.

LOOKING REFLECTIVELY

I am so thankful God doesn't hold our sin against us if we've put our faith in Jesus as our Savior. Even though God has forgiven us for all our sins through Christ's death on the cross, we still need to confess as we commit sins each day. Unconfessed sin hinders our fellowship with God. Pray that God would keep you sensitive to the Holy Spirit convicting you of sin so you can deal with it immediately. God doesn't show us our sin to discourage us, but to make us aware of it so we can confess it and move forward in close fellowship with Him.

- Is there unconfessed sin in your life? Confess it. Thank God for His forgiveness. Ask Him to help you turn away from it.
- In what ways have you seen God instruct, teach, lead, and redirect you?
- Use Psalm 130 to guide you through a time of prayer and confession today.

"Lord Jesus, I sin—Grant that I may never cease grieving because of it, never be content with myself, never think I can reach a point of perfection. Kill my envy, command my tongue, trample down self. Give me grace to be holy, kind, gentle, pure, peaceable, to live for thee and not for self, to copy thy words, acts, spirit, to be transformed into thy likeness, to be consecrated wholly to thee, to live entirely to thy glory."[4]

FROM *THE VALLEY OF VISION*

MY EYES ARE CONTINUALLY TOWARD THE LORD

We are instructed throughout the Bible to fear the Lord. That doesn't mean we should be afraid of God but should revere Him and stand before Him in awe. When we fear God, we want to please Him and bring Him glory, not dishonor and disappointment. David talks about fearing God in today's lesson. He points out in this psalm that when we fear God, our eyes are continually toward the Lord. Where are your eyes focused today?

Father, I want to fear You and bow before You. Teach me what that means and how I can live it out. Help me keep my eyes continually toward You.

LOOKING TO GOD'S WORD
PSALM 25:12–15

1. Today we're going to focus on verses 12–15. Mark in the introductory paragraph above what it means to fear God (v. 12). What would you add to that?

2. According to verses 12–14, what are the results of fearing God?

3. What does David mean by "the secret of the LORD" in verse 14?

4. David says, "My eyes are continually toward the LORD" in verse 15. What does that imply about David's relationship with God?

5. How does David express his confidence in God?

LOOKING UPWARD

6. What are some things that tempt us to take our eyes off the Lord?

7. How can we keep our eyes on Him? What are some habits that will help us?

LOOKING DEEPER

8. What additional insights do these verses give concerning fear of the Lord?

- Job 28:28

- Psalm 31:19

- Psalm 111:10

- Proverbs 1:7

LOOKING REFLECTIVELY

I am thankful I can come boldly before God at any time, pouring out my heart, being honest with how and what I'm feeling. But I pray I'd not lose that sense of awe in who He is—the Creator, the Sovereign God, the Holy One. Just knowing that He wants a personal relationship with me brings me to my knees in awe of His great love.

- Do you fear God in the sense of its biblical meaning? Do you revere Him in awe?
- If not, what is hindering you? What can you do to grow in this area?
- Are your eyes continually toward the Lord? If not, where are they focused? What do you need to do to get your eyes back on the Lord?
- Use David's prayer in 1 Chronicles 29:10–13 to lead you through a time of praise and worship. Write out a prayer here or in your journal.

"When you pray, fix your eyes, as David did, on the fact that God is: good, upright, willing to instruct sinners, loving, faithful, forgiving. What confidence we can have in prayer, not because we pray well, but because of the nature of the God to whom we pray."[5]

LAWRENCE O. RICHARDS

I TAKE REFUGE IN YOU

There are times we just want to escape and get away from the stresses of life and the problems we're facing. We sometimes don't know how we're going to get through a difficult situation. The answer? Turn to God and ask Him for help. Today we finish looking at Psalm 25. David is honest with God about his feelings and fears. He turns to God and asks for His help and grace to get through hard times. Regardless of what we're going through, God is with us every step of the way. Cling to Him!

Lord, I need You. I can't get through this on my own. You know the way. You know what's around the corner. Strengthen me. Be gracious to me. Hold my hand tightly in Yours.

LOOKING TO GOD'S WORD
PSALM 25:16–22

1. Describe David's state of mind. What is he feeling? What is he going through?

2. There are at least eight prayer requests of David in this section. List them.

3. Why do you think he adds the prayer for redeeming Israel "out of all his troubles" in verse 22?

4. How does this final section compare to the first section of this psalm (Day 1)?

5. As you look back over Psalm 25, how would you summarize David's view of God?

LOOKING UPWARD

6. How would "integrity and uprightness" preserve us (v. 21)?

7. Can you give an example of a time when you felt lonely or distressed? How did you approach God in prayer? How did He respond to you?

LOOKING DEEPER

As you read Psalm 25 again, identify the seven components of the lament listed below, and write the verse number by each. Remember, not all seven parts are found in every lament, and they are not necessarily in the following order, but there will always be a complaint.

   1. An address to God
   2. A review of God's faithfulness in the past
   3. A complaint
   4. A confession of sin or claim of innocence
   5. A request for help
   6. God's response
   7. A vow to praise God or a statement of trust in God

LOOKING REFLECTIVELY

I wrote my first lament psalm to the Lord several years ago when I attended an equipping conference for trauma healing hosted by the American Bible Society. I hadn't gone through any trauma, so I approached this class as simply training to equip me to help those who have. When we got to the section about the lament, we were given time alone to write a lament to God, and it was life-changing for me.

I realized as I poured out my heart to Him on paper, I had hurts I had not expressed to anyone. As I wrote the lament psalm to God, the tears came, but also a peace that my loving God is in control. He knows what I'm feeling. It was a powerful exercise, and I've continued to write lament psalms to the Lord when I find myself discouraged and weary.

Take some time today to write a lament psalm to the Lord below or in your prayer journal. You don't have to include all seven components, but you need to express your complaint (hurt/trouble/stress). You will find God takes you to a deeper place with Him as you pour out your heart and, at the same time, express trust in Him.

_____

_____

_____

_____

_____

_____

_____

"I love the word pour. I picture a giant pitcher with all my worries, cares, frets, and burns pouring out into your hands. I choose to pour everything out to you right now, Jesus. Please take my fear. Please take the difficult relationships in my life. Please receive my worry about provision. Please hold my wayward friends and loved ones. Please absorb my confusion and bewilderment. Thank you that you truly are my refuge, my shelter, and my safe house. . . . I need you, Jesus."[6]

MARY DEMUTH

ASA:
A PRAYER OF
SEEKING GOD

The morning of December 19, 2014, will forever be etched in my memory. That morning, I sat beside my mom's bed and watched her take her last breath and step into the presence of the Lord. I could only imagine the celebration going on in heaven, and I could picture Jesus telling her, *Well done, Marjorie. You finished well.*

Mom was a godly example to me over the years. She was teaching Sunday school well into her 80s until her eyesight began to fail. When she moved into assisted living, she was faithful to attend the Bible studies and church services there. She was an encouragement to everyone around her. Even in her final years when she couldn't talk, hear, or see, Mom still ministered to others and showed the love of Christ by her smile. Mom finished well.

How do you want your life to look at the end of your earthly journey? Will you finish strong for the Lord, or will you drift away from your devotion to Christ? How are you living your life today? Are you more confident in your own abilities and leaning less on the Lord, or are you consistently seeking Him? The key to finishing well is continuously seeking the Lord in all things, not relying on your own strength or earthly wisdom.

This week we are going to study King Asa. He began well, but he didn't finish well. A key phrase found in Asa's story is "seek the LORD." When he sought the Lord, God granted him favor and success. When he stopped seeking God, his life changed, and not for the better. Let's learn from Asa's life.

THE SETTING

Asa was the third king of Judah, and he reigned for forty-one years. He started out well, making wise decisions as he sought the Lord in difficult circumstances. He's considered to be one of the better kings over Judah as he carried out numerous reforms. Today we'll look at the early years of his reign and the strength of his relationship with God.

Lord, I know I'm weak apart from You. Protect me from becoming complacent, proud, and self-reliant. Remind me of my dependence on You and my need to seek You continually. Teach me from the example of Asa and his prayer to You in a time of great need.

LOOKING TO GOD'S WORD
2 CHRONICLES 14:1–8

1. What do you learn about Asa in verses 1–2?

2. What did he accomplish in his early years as king (verses 3–6)?

3. How did he demonstrate wisdom during this time?

4. What was this season like for the nation of Judah?

5. List any other observations from this passage that stand out to you and why.

We are told in verses 3 and 5 that Asa removed the high places. It's important to understand why that was a significant accomplishment for Asa during his rule. "High place" is translated from the Hebrew word *bāmâ*. It was a place of worship, located on a hilltop or manmade platform, and was usually associated with pagan religious practices. The land was flat, and the people thought the gods lived in the heavens above. So they believed an elevated place of worship had a better chance of gaining the attention of the gods.[1] Asa wanted to remove these high places that could tempt his people to worship the pagan gods.

LOOKING UPWARD

6. Verse 7 tells us Asa and the people of Judah sought the LORD. What does it mean to seek the Lord?

7. How do you seek the Lord? What helps you to do so?

8. What hinders you from seeking God?

LOOKING DEEPER

David wrote Psalm 63 in the wilderness of Judah while he was running from Saul. Although he was away from the ark of God and the formal place of worship, he still longed to worship. We get a glimpse into David's heart as he expressed his longing for God in this psalm.

9. Read Psalm 63. How did David seek God and express his need for God?

10. Write down any other thoughts you have about this psalm.

LOOKING REFLECTIVELY

Asa tore down the idols and removed the high places because he wanted to rid Judah of idolatry. We tend to think of idolatry as worshiping the statues of false gods, so we don't typically consider ourselves to be idolaters. But we are all guilty of idolatry in some form. We may not worship statues, but we find ourselves worshiping other things that become more important to us than God.

- What do you most seek in life—God, material possessions, money, status, or something else?
- What are the potential idols in your life—your job, your children, your spouse, prestige, money, possessions, other things?
- Are there any idols already in your life you need to tear down?
- Use Psalm 63 to guide you through a time of prayer. You may want to write a prayer below or in your prayer journal as you ponder the questions above.

"What is an idol? It is anything more important to you than God, anything that absorbs your heart and imagination more than God, anything you seek to give you what only God can give."[2]

TIMOTHY KELLER

THE PRAYER

How do you respond when an overwhelming situation arises? Do you try to handle it on your own, or do you seek God? Asa gives us a great example to follow when life comes at us unexpectedly. He turned to prayer. Today we're going to look at his short, but powerful, prayer and how he viewed God.

Lord, there are days I am caught off guard by unexpected things. Help me turn to You in prayer and recognize I can't handle these overwhelming situations on my own. Nothing is too difficult for You, and I rest in Your power and strength to handle the impossible. Thank You, Lord.

LOOKING TO GOD'S WORD
2 CHRONICLES 14:9–15

1. What was the situation in verses 9–10 that prompted Asa to call out to the Lord his God? How did the two armies differ (vv. 8–9)?

2. How would you describe Asa's prayer in verse 11?

3. How does he begin his prayer?

4. What is his attitude in approaching God?

5. What does he ask for?

6. How does God answer his prayer (v. 12)?

7. What were the results of this battle (vv. 13–15)?

LOOKING UPWARD

8. Give an example of a time when you felt weak and helpless apart from the Lord's strength. How did you respond to God? How did you see Him work?

LOOKING DEEPER

Asa was facing an overwhelming situation, and he turned to God for help. David often found himself in situations where he faced overwhelming battles, and he also turned to God in prayer. Psalm 20 records one of David's prayers for victory over his enemies.

9. Read David's prayer in Psalm 20. In the New American Standard Bible (NASB), David begins seven sentences with the word "may." List David's requests below. (If you don't have the NASB, go to biblegateway.com and select that version for Psalm 20 to make your list.)

10. What stands out to you about David's prayer?

11. How is David's prayer similar to Asa's prayer?

LOOKING REFLECTIVELY

One of the shortest prayers I've prayed (and continue to pray) is, "Help me, Lord."
Our prayers don't have to be long and eloquent to be effective. That's one of the
reasons I love Asa's prayer. Even though it's short, he says much in these few words.
He admits his inadequacy and expresses his confidence and trust in God to help.
Make Asa's prayer in 2 Chronicles 14:11 your prayer today. Pray his words back to
the Lord in your own words, according to your specific situation. You may want to
write out your prayer below or in your prayer journal and look at it again later.

*"Whether we praise him for his unfathomable majesty or petition him for daily
needs, prayer is the expression of our dependence upon God, our whole-souled
reliance upon his power to sustain us, his mercy to forgive us, his bounty to
supply us, and his glory to overwhelm us as we reflect on who he is."*[3]

C. SAMUEL STORMS

THE EXHORTATION

Encouragement is good for the soul. When we do things well, it's nice to hear affirmation and words that spur us on to keep doing what we're doing. We also need people who are willing to speak truth to us and warn us of dangerous paths we might be tempted to take. In today's passage, God sent His prophet Azariah to encourage Asa in his work. He exhorted him to keep seeking God. We all need an "Azariah" in our lives.

> *Father, it's easy to get weary and discouraged in the work You've called me to do. Bring people around me to encourage and spur me on. Keep me teachable to their words of exhortation. Make me sensitive to those around me who need an encouraging word.*

LOOKING TO GOD'S WORD
2 CHRONICLES 15:1–19

1. Read 2 Chronicles 15:1–7. What is the message Azariah wanted to get across to Asa?

2. Azariah's words to Asa were both an encouragement and a warning. In what ways were they an encouragement?

3. In what ways were Azariah's words a warning?

4. Read 2 Chronicles 15:8–19. How did Asa respond to Azariah's prophecy? List all he did.

5. Describe Judah's heart toward God in verses 9–15.

6. What do you observe about seeking the Lord in 2 Chronicles 15:1–19? What was the result of their seeking God?

7. How would you describe Asa at this point in his life?

LOOKING UPWARD

8. According to 2 Chronicles 15:17, "Asa's heart was blameless all his days." This doesn't mean he didn't sin, but most scholars agree this verse is a general summary of his life. Overall, he was a good king who followed God. What can we learn from Asa's life up to this point that would help us live blameless lives?

LOOKING DEEPER

2 Chronicles 15:17 has raised some questions about the high places: "But the high places were not removed from Israel . . ." Yet 2 Chronicles 14:5 tells us, "He also removed the high places and the incense altars from all the cities of Judah." Rather than this being a contradiction, it is more likely that the writer is referring to Asa removing all the high places of Judah but not in Israel.[4]

We can become discouraged in doing the work of the Lord. Azariah encouraged Asa in 2 Chronicles 15:1–7. Paul gave the Corinthians similar encouragement in 1 Corinthians 15:58. Are you discouraged today? Do you wonder if what you're doing is really worth it, and is it making any difference?

9. Write out 2 Chronicles 15:7 and 1 Corinthians 15:58 in your own words.

10. How do those verses encourage you today? How can you use them to encourage someone else?

LOOKING REFLECTIVELY

Azariah admonished Asa to keep seeking God and not put his confidence in himself. That's a good message for all of us. When we see victory, we're sometimes tempted to believe we can do life on our own and don't need God's help. But we should heed Azariah's admonition to Asa and keep looking to God for strength, guidance, and help. We will never be sufficient on our own.

Asa and the nation of Judah sought the Lord God of their fathers with all their heart and soul. How would you describe your relationship with God? Are you seeking Him with all your heart? Through prayer or journaling, be honest with God about where you are with Him.

- Are you seeking the Lord in prayer and through His Word? Are you spending consistent time alone with Him? If not, what steps can you take to protect that time with Him?
- Is pride keeping you from seeking the Lord? If so, confess it.
- Spend some time in prayer. What do you need to seek Him for today? Wisdom in a decision? Strength in a difficult situation? Grace to forgive someone? Journal your thoughts.

"Seeking involves calling and pleading. 'O Lord, open my eyes. O Lord, pull back the curtain of my own blindness. Lord, have mercy and reveal yourself. I long to see your face.' The great obstacle to seeking the Lord is pride. 'In the pride of his face the wicked does not seek him' (Psalm 10:4). Therefore, humility is essential to seeking the Lord."[5]

JOHN PIPER

A TURNING POINT

Most of us can look back and pinpoint a turning point in our lives—a time we made a decision that changed the direction of our lives. Sometimes such turning points move us in a better direction. Other times, they direct us down the wrong path. Today we're going to look at a turning point in Asa's life in 2 Chronicles 16 and how he changed compared to who he was at the beginning of his reign as king of Judah.

God, You know the path You want me on. Keep me from wandering off in my own direction. Keep me attentive to Your Word and the prompting of Your Holy Spirit in me. Show me Your way, Lord. I want to continually seek You.

LOOKING TO GOD'S WORD
2 CHRONICLES 16:1–14

1. Read 2 Chronicles 16:1–6. Describe the situation and when this happened.

2. What was different this time in the way Asa dealt with the situation? How did he change from the beginning of his rule over Judah? (Look again at 2 Chronicles 14:9–11.)

3. Read 2 Chronicles 16:7–14. How did the seer Hanani confront Asa in verses 7–9?

4. How did Asa respond to the rebuke in verse 10? What does this reveal about Asa at this time?

5. Describe the end of Asa's life in verses 11–14.

LOOKING UPWARD

6. Why would we stop seeking the Lord after seeing God's hand work so powerfully in other situations?

7. What lessons can we learn from the life of Asa?

LOOKING DEEPER

8. Read Jeremiah 17:5–8. Contrast the man who trusts in himself or others with the man who trusts in God. Write down your thoughts from this passage.

LOOKING REFLECTIVELY

When I accepted the job as the Women's Ministry Director at a church in Memphis, I shared with the placement director of Dallas Theological Seminary how excited I was. But I also told him I was scared to death! *What if I can't do the job? What if I fail? What if I disappoint them?*

He responded, "That's a great place to be because it will keep you flat on your face before God the first few years of your ministry there. And if you're wise, you will stay in that position the rest of your life." I have never forgotten his words.

We all face the temptation to look to others or to ourselves for strength and guidance, as Asa did, and we stop seeking the Lord. I don't want to start out well but then not finish well because I lost that sense of total dependence on God.

- Spend some time in prayer with the Father. He knows all things—what's ahead, the outcome, the lessons to be learned. Bow before Him—either with bowed head, on your knees, or face down on the floor. Acknowledge who He is. Focus on His attributes. Worship Him.
- Ask Him to show you any unconfessed sin in your heart—pride, worry, fear, jealousy, critical spirit, self-sufficiency, other sins. Confess it.
- Ask God to show you if you're looking to any source for strength, protection, and guidance other than God first and foremost. If so, confess it. Seek the Lord.

"The eternal, sovereign, majestic God of the universe wants to be intimate with us! He wants us to call, to cry, to sing to Him. He longs to love, to refresh, to encourage us. He wants to answer our call and to tell us great and unsearchable thoughts."[6]

CYNTHIA HEALD

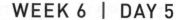

ANOTHER PRAYER OF SEEKING GOD

Asa began well as king of Judah as he sought the Lord in every situation. But later, he turned to other people instead of seeking God. As a result, he didn't finish strong. Today we're going to look at a prayer of David in Psalm 27. This is an example of how we should pray when circumstances remind us of our inadequacy; an example of how Asa should have prayed later in his life. Psalm 27 is one of my favorite psalms, and I continue to go back to it when life seems overwhelming and fears creep in.

Lord, I want to seek You first and foremost. Yet I know there
are times I look to others, or even myself. Forgive me when I do.
Remind me of my inadequacy and Your sufficiency. Help me
continue to seek You and You alone.

LOOKING TO GOD'S WORD
PSALM 27

1. Read Psalm 27 aloud. Describe David's heart in this prayer.

2. Why is David confident in God? How does he express this confidence and trust?

3. What are the two things David said "I shall seek" in verses 4 and 8? What does that tell us about David's relationship with God?

4. Why would he seek them instead of material things or honor?

5. What does David ask of God in this psalm? List his requests.

LOOKING UPWARD

6. In verse 14, David talks about waiting for God. What is the relationship between waiting on God and seeking His face?

7. How would these requests have also been applicable for Asa to pray during his reign?

LOOKING DEEPER

8. What do these verses say about seeking God?

- 1 Chronicles 16:11

- 1 Chronicles 22:19

• Psalm 9:10

• Psalm 105:4

9. What stands out to you from these verses?

LOOKING REFLECTIVELY

Asa started out well as king of Judah. He wanted to please God by tearing down the idols and high places. In his earlier years, he sought God in prayer, knowing his only hope was in God. But he didn't finish well because he stopped seeking God and began looking to others for help.

- As you look back over your life, have there been times when you stopped seeking the Lord and looked to other things or people for answers, guidance, or strength? What were the results?
- Is there someone you know who has stopped seeking God and is drifting away? Pray for them now. Ask God to show you how you can be an Azariah in their life.
- What a privilege we have to be able to go to God in prayer at any time. He delights when we come to Him in prayer to seek Him. Sing and ponder the words of the hymn "Sweet Hour of Prayer."[7]

Sweet hour of prayer! Sweet hour of prayer!
That calls me from a world of care,
And bids me at my Father's throne
Make all my wants and wishes known.
In seasons of distress and grief,

My soul has often found relief,
And oft escaped the tempter's snare
By thy return, sweet hour of prayer!

Sweet hour of prayer! Sweet hour of prayer!
The joys I feel, the bliss I share
Of those whose anxious spirits burn
With strong desires for thy return!
With such I hasten to the place
Where God my Savior shows His face,
And gladly take my station there,
And wait for thee, sweet hour of prayer!

Sweet hour of prayer! Sweet hour of prayer!
Thy wings shall my petition bear
To Him whose truth and faithfulness
Engage the waiting soul to bless.
And since He bids me seek His face,
Believe His Word, and trust His grace,
I'll cast on Him my every care,
And wait for thee, sweet hour of prayer!

Write your own psalm about seeking God below or in your prayer journal. Use David's example in Psalm 27 to guide you.

_____

_____

_____

_____

_____

_____

_____

_____

"Through prayer we commune with God; we align ourselves with his purposes. We learn the sound of his voice. We discover his power and learn to trust his promises. . . . We learn to submit to God's greater wisdom and knowledge."[8]

JAN WINEBRENNER

JEHOSHAPHAT: A PRAYER OF DEPENDENCE

We all have those days when life seems overwhelming and out of control. Responsibilities grow, deadlines loom, people need to be seen, and unexpected surprises interrupt the plans for the day. When life feels out of control, fear creeps in. *How am I going to get everything done, Lord? How am I going to deal with this situation? I don't know what to do.* We may feel hopeless and powerless. Yet it is in those times of desperation when the Lord meets us in a special way as we cry out to Him in prayer.

That is the situation with Asa's son, King Jehoshaphat, in this week's lesson. He was king of Judah, and things had gone well for him. But now he faced a situation that brought him to his knees, and he turned to the Lord and cried for help. What did he learn from watching his father Asa? What a great example his prayer is for us as we find ourselves overwhelmed and scared, and we recognize our inadequacy.

THE BEGINNING OF JEHOSHAPHAT'S REIGN

Jehoshaphat did a lot of things right as king of Judah and set a positive example for the people. He loved God and wanted to honor Him. In today's lesson, we're going to look at the beginning of his reign and how he led the nation of Judah. As we begin this new week, thank God for His faithfulness in the past and for His continued guidance in every circumstance.

Father, I know there are going to be those days when I don't know how to handle a situation. Thank You that I can come to You at all times and look to You for guidance, strength, and peace. Keep my eyes focused on You. May I be an example to others of how to walk with You.

LOOKING TO GOD'S WORD
2 CHRONICLES 17

1. Read 2 Chronicles 17 and mark any words or phrases that stand out to you.

2. What are some of the positives and strengths that characterized Jehoshaphat's reign over Judah?

3. How would you describe his relationship with God?

Close, loyal

4. What are some things he did that demonstrated his commitment to God?

5. How did the surrounding nations view Judah and Jehoshaphat (vv. 10–11)?

LOOKING UPWARD

6. 2 Chronicles 17:6 tells us Jehoshaphat "took great pride in the ways of the LORD." What does that mean? What would that look like for you?

LOOKING DEEPER

7. What additional information does 1 Kings 22:41–50 give concerning Jehoshaphat?

LOOKING REFLECTIVELY

Seeking God is critical to a fruitful ministry and godly leadership, as we saw with Asa. Jehoshaphat sought the LORD and was obedient to Him. He also sent men to teach God's Word throughout Judah, he removed the high places, and he followed the example of the earlier days of David and Asa. Jehoshaphat was a godly leader.

- Are you seeking God in everything you do? In decisions you're making? If not, what is hindering you from seeking Him?
- How can you use God's Word to spur others on in their faith?
- What kind of example are you setting for your children, grandchildren, nieces and nephews, and others who are watching you? Is there anything you're doing that you would not want them to do?
- Spend some time with the Lord in prayer as you ponder these questions.

"Oh, teach us to know you, our God, and enable us to do your will as we ought to do. Give us hearts to love you, to trust and delight in you. That no temptations may draw us, nor any tribulations drive us from you; but that all your dispensations to us, and all your dealings with us, may be the messengers of your love to our souls, to bring us still nearer to your blessed self, and to make us still fitter for your heavenly kingdom." [1]

BENJAMIN JENKS

A DIFFICULT SITUATION

Have you ever faced a difficult situation that seemed overwhelming and you were not sure how you were going to get through it? I have. When I try to handle it on my own, I am worried and anxious, and sometimes I make poor decisions. But, when I turn it over to God through prayer, He gives me guidance and peace.

Life was going great for Jehoshaphat in the beginning of his reign over Judah. But he made an unwise decision by partnering with Ahab, king of Israel, through marriage (2 Chronicles 18). We see his teachable heart as he responded positively to Jehu's rebuke in 2 Chronicles 19. As we pick up the story in chapter 20, Jehoshaphat is faced with a difficult situation that drew him into a desperate dependence on God. He didn't try to handle it on his own, and that's a great lesson for us.

Father, as much as I dislike overwhelming situations in life,
You use those times to show me my need for You and how powerful
You are to handle anything that comes my way. Thank You for
deepening my faith each time I face challenges in life.

LOOKING TO GOD'S WORD
2 CHRONICLES 20:1-4

1. Verse 1 begins with "Now it came about after this . . ." What is "this" referring to? (Look back at the context in chapter 19.)

2. How would you describe Jehoshaphat and his relationship with God at this point in his reign?

3. What was the situation Jehoshaphat was facing in 2 Chronicles 20:1–2?

4. How did Jehoshaphat respond to this situation (v. 3)? What was the progression of his response?

5. How did the people of Judah respond in verse 4? What does that indicate about Judah?

6. Why do you think they chose to gather together instead of staying in their cities?

LOOKING UPWARD

7. Jehoshaphat was afraid (v. 3). Are we sinning when we are afraid and fearful? Explain your answer.

8. Describe a situation in which you were afraid or fearful. How did you respond? What did you learn from it?

LOOKING DEEPER

Fear is something we all deal with. Throughout the Bible, we are commanded to "fear not." Fear can be our greatest friend or our greatest enemy. It can be our greatest friend if we allow it to move us to our knees to seek God's strength and help. It can be our greatest enemy if we allow it to paralyze us and keep us from stepping out in faith to follow God's leading.

9. One of my favorite "fear" passages is Isaiah 41:10. Write this verse below.

#102 - quite a promise

10. What are the commands?

11. What are the reasons given for why we shouldn't fear?

LOOKING REFLECTIVELY

I've had my share of times when I felt fearful about something—fear of the future, fear of the unknown, fear of rejection, fear of failure. Those fears would have paralyzed me if I had not taken them before the Lord and looked to Him for strength and confidence.

- How have you handled your times of fear? What did you learn in those times?
- Is something making you afraid and fearful today? Meditate on Psalm 91. Why should we not be fearful? What do you learn about God from this psalm? Make it your prayer.

"The moment I feel fear, that should be the signal to trust; and once I put my trust in God, I must dismiss my fear and calmly move forward."[2]

W. GLYN EVANS

THE DISCIPLINE
OF FASTING

Many of us don't practice the discipline of fasting as they did in the Old Testament, but why don't we? The Bible doesn't say it's obsolete now that Jesus has come. Jesus Himself often spoke about fasting when He was on this earth. What is the purpose of it? Why should we as Christians fast, and when should we fast?

Jehoshaphat proclaimed a fast throughout all Judah, and the people did as Jehoshaphat asked. We don't read in Scripture that they complained or asked why. We are simply told, "So Judah gathered together to seek help from the LORD; they even came from all the cities of Judah to seek the LORD" (2 Chron. 20:4).

Today we're going to look closer at this area of fasting. Why did Jehoshaphat call his people to fast? What other godly men called for a fast and why? Ask God to show you the importance and value of fasting when done with the right motives.

Father, I confess I don't often fast with prayer. Yet we see
throughout Scripture the examples of godly leaders fasting.
Help me see the value of this spiritual discipline and
give me a desire to practice it more often.

LOOKING TO GOD'S WORD
2 CHRONICLES 20:3-4

1. Read 2 Chronicles 20:3–4. Why did Jehoshaphat proclaim a fast throughout Judah? What was the purpose?

2. What do you observe about fasting and its purpose in the following passages? Write down anything that stands out to you.

Ezra 8:21–23 (ESV)

Then I proclaimed a fast there, at the river Ahava, that we might humble ourselves before our God, to seek from him a safe journey for ourselves, our children, and all our goods. For I was ashamed to ask the king for a band of soldiers and horsemen to protect us against the enemy on our way, since we had told the king, "The hand of our God is for good on all who seek him, and the power of his wrath is against all who forsake him." So we fasted and implored our God for this, and he listened to our entreaty.

1 Samuel 7:3–6 (ESV)

And Samuel said to all the house of Israel, "If you are returning to the Lord with all your heart, then put away the foreign gods and the Ashtaroth from among you and direct your heart to the Lord and serve him only, and he will deliver you out of the hand of the Philistines." So the people of Israel put away the Baals and the Ashtaroth, and they served the Lord only. Then Samuel said, "Gather all Israel at Mizpah, and I will pray to the Lord for you." So they gathered at Mizpah and drew water and poured it out before the Lord and fasted on that day and said there, "We have sinned against the Lord." And Samuel judged the people of Israel at Mizpah.

Nehemiah 9:1–4 (ESV)

Now on the twenty-fourth day of this month the people of Israel were assembled with fasting and in sackcloth, and with earth on their heads. And the Israelites separated themselves from all foreigners and stood and confessed their sins and the iniquities of their fathers. And they stood up in their place and read from the Book of the Law of the LORD their God for a quarter of the day; for another quarter of it they made confession and worshiped the LORD their God. On the stairs of the Levites stood Jeshua, Bani, Kadmiel, Shebaniah, Bunni, Sherebiah, Bani, and Chenani; and they cried with a loud voice to the LORD their God.

Jonah 3:4–9 (ESV)

Jonah began to go into the city, going a day's journey. And he called out, "Yet forty days, and Nineveh shall be overthrown!" And the people of Nineveh believed God. They called for a fast and put on sackcloth, from the greatest of them to the least of them. The word reached the king of Nineveh, and he arose from his throne, removed his robe, covered himself with sackcloth, and sat in ashes. And he issued a proclamation and published through Nineveh, "By the decree of the king and his nobles: Let neither man nor beast, herd nor flock, taste anything. Let them not feed or drink water, but let man and beast be covered with sackcloth, and let them call out mightily to God. Let everyone turn from his evil way and from the violence that is in his hands. Who knows? God may turn and relent and turn from his fierce anger, so that we may not perish."

3. What was the purpose of sackcloth and ashes in fasting?

LOOKING UPWARD

4. How would fasting help us seek the Lord? How would it strengthen our prayers?

Spiritual discipline besides prayer X

5. Why is fasting a way of humbling ourselves before God?

6. Does our fasting move God to answer our prayers in the way we desire? Why or why not?

LOOKING DEEPER

7. What does Jesus say about fasting in Matthew 6:16–18? What observations can you make from this passage about fasting?

LOOKING REFLECTIVELY

I admit I don't regularly fast, but I have done it on a number of occasions. Each time, it has been a sweet time of communion and intimacy with the Lord. Usually, I have fasted and prayed when my heart was burdened to spend some extended time in prayer about something specific.

What keeps you from fasting?

If you have fasted with prayer, what did you see God do as a result? What did you learn from that time?

Is there something you need to pray and fast about this week? You may want to fast from all water and food or just fast from food or a certain type of food. You can do a partial fast where you only eat or drink certain things (like fruit or juice). You may want to fast for just one meal or fast until sundown. As you fast, spend time in prayer. This discipline of fasting will deepen your time with God.

How hungry are you for God? Do you long to know more of Him? Do you long for Him to be your sufficiency in whatever situation He has you? Journal your thoughts.

"There's something about fasting that sharpens the edge of our intercessions and gives passion to our supplications. So it has frequently been used by the people of God when there is a special urgency about the concerns they lift before the Father."[3]

DONALD WHITNEY

JEHOSHAPHAT'S PRAYER

There are times we think we have everything under control, but then God puts us in a situation to remind us we don't. We need Him. A situation arose that drew Jehoshaphat into a desperate dependence on God, and he turned to God in prayer. As much as we dislike overwhelming situations, God uses them to show us our need for Him and how powerful He is.

Today we're going to look at Jehoshaphat's prayer which shows his desperate dependence on God. His prayer was longer than his father Asa's, but the length of our prayers isn't what matters. What's important is the attitude with which we approach God in prayer.

> *Lord, teach me to pray as Jehoshaphat did. Remind me that nothing*
> *is too difficult for You. Help me keep my eyes on You, not the*
> *circumstances surrounding me.*

LOOKING TO GOD'S WORD
2 CHRONICLES 20:5-13

1. Describe Jehoshaphat's prayer. What are the components of His prayer?

2. How does he describe and view God? What do you learn about his relationship with God?

3. In verse 7, he asks God a question to which he already knew the answer. What would be the purpose of doing this?

4. What stands out to you about Jehoshaphat's prayer and the way he approached God?

LOOKING UPWARD

5. Jehoshaphat focused on God for power and strength, not on himself. That's how we should respond when we feel powerless and don't know what to do. Why do we often still try to get through those fearful and overwhelming situations on our own strength instead of looking to God?

LOOKING DEEPER

6. In 2 Chronicles 20:12, Jehoshaphat prayed, ". . . nor do we know what to do, but our eyes are on You." Read Psalm 121, a psalm of ascent. Why should we look to God?

LOOKING REFLECTIVELY

Several things stand out to me as I look at Jehoshaphat's prayer: (1) He recognized his inadequacy to deal with the situation. "For we are powerless . . ." He knew he needed God's help and couldn't handle this on his own strength. (2) He knew what he was up against. ". . . before this great multitude who are coming against us." Jehoshaphat didn't minimize the problem or ignore it, but he acknowledged how great the problem was. (3) He admitted his need for help. "Nor do we know what to do." It's okay to admit we don't know what to do in an overwhelming situation. (4) He handled his need in the right way—he looked to the Lord for help. "Our eyes are on You."

I have often said the words, "Lord, I don't know what to do . . ." And He always reminds me of Jehoshaphat's prayer, ". . . but our eyes are on You." How have you seen God use challenging situations to draw you into a deeper dependence on Him?

Are you facing a situation today that seems overwhelming? Are you fearful of something? Do you need wisdom and guidance? Be honest with God about it.

Spend some time in prayer using Psalm 121 to guide you. Write a prayer below or in your journal based on Psalm 121.

"Trust in the LORD with all your heart, and do not lean on your own understanding. In all your ways acknowledge him, and he will make straight your paths."

SOLOMON (PROVERBS 3:5–6 ESV)

GOD'S ANSWER

When we find ourselves in an overwhelming situation, we cry out to God and wait for Him to answer. Sometimes we see His answer immediately, and it may not always be what we had hoped for. But He knows what He's doing in the bigger scheme of things. Sometimes we have to wait for God to answer in His timing, not ours. It's not easy to wait, but God is at work in ways we can't see. Other times, we see His hand at work in ways that bring us to our knees in praise and worship. "God, only You could have done this!"

> *Lord, You want me to cry out to You in prayer. When life comes at me hard and fast, and I don't know what to do, remind me of my need to look to You. Help me praise You as I see You work, even if it's different than the way I had hoped. Help me rest in Your sovereignty.*

LOOKING TO GOD'S WORD
2 CHRONICLES 20:14–25

1. How did God respond to the prayers of Jehoshaphat and the people of Judah?

2. What were the instructions for the people of Judah to follow in this battle? Why do you think God orchestrated the battle in this way?

3. Why do you think they responded to God in the way they did in verses 18–19?

4. What do you observe about the way Jehoshaphat handled the situation in verses 20–21?

5. How did God defeat their enemies?

LOOKING UPWARD

6. How did you see God fight your battles for you today? Can you give a specific example?

7. Read 2 Chronicles 20 again and write down all the ways Jehoshaphat showed his dependence on God.

LOOKING DEEPER

God delights to fight our battles for us. He doesn't want us to move forward in our own strength, but to rely solely on Him. There are numerous examples of this in the Old Testament (Ex. 14:10–18; Josh. 6:1–26; Judg. 7:1–23).

8. Look at Exodus 14:10–18 when God used Moses to lead the sons of Israel out of captivity in Egypt through the Red Sea. How were they dependent on God for victory?

9. List your observations about how God fought the battle for His people and led them to victory.

LOOKING REFLECTIVELY

Jehoshaphat's prayer is one of my favorite prayers in the Bible. The first time I prayed this prayer was shortly after I went on staff with Campus Crusade for Christ (now called Cru) over thirty-five years ago. I was in the process of putting together my support team—financial and prayer—and had just come home from an appointment with a person I had known many years. I was certain she would immediately jump on board to be part of my support team.

Instead, it was a devastating conversation. She wanted nothing to do with supporting me financially or through prayer. Leaving in tears, I went home, shut the door to my room, and got on my knees. I began questioning if God wanted me on staff with Campus Crusade, as I wasn't getting very far with my support, and I had a large amount to raise. I didn't see any way it could be done.

I opened my Bible to 2 Chronicles 20:5–12 and read Jehoshaphat's prayer. Tears fell on the words in my Bible, and I cried out to God for help and direction. "God, I don't know what to do, but my eyes are on You. Show me, Lord."

The next day, I got a phone call from a man in another city whom I had met the previous week. He called to tell me he wanted to be part of my team, and the large amount he pledged sent me back to my knees in awe of God's power. God used this man's response to confirm I was moving in the right direction. I never questioned God's calling for me after that, even though there were other times of discouragement. But He always answered my cry for help.

- How have you seen God fight for you and take care of you in overwhelming circumstances?
- Are you in the middle of a discouraging situation today? Are you feeling

overwhelmed? Weak? Write a prayer to God, expressing your feelings. Cry out to Him, "Lord, I don't know what to do, but my eyes are on You." Wait and see how God works.

- How are you expressing your dependence on God today?
- Spend some time in prayer, using Jehoshaphat's prayer in 2 Chronicles 20:5–12 to guide you. Write your prayer in the space below or in your prayer journal.

_____

_____

_____

_____

_____

_____

_____

_____

*"Prayer is not so much an act as it is an attitude—
an attitude of dependency; dependency upon God."* [4]

ARTHUR W. PINK

NEHEMIAH: A PRAYER OF BOLDNESS

I confess, I'm not good at asking God for what seems impossible. Perhaps it's because my faith isn't strong enough or because I only pray for things I can easily see accomplished. I hate to think of what I am missing by not boldly asking God for things only He can do.

Even this morning as I was praying, I realized I wasn't asking God to handle a tough situation because I felt it was too overwhelming! God showed me I wasn't believing He could do anything, no matter how impossible it seems. I need to grow in this area of prayer.

Nehemiah is a great example of what it means to pray boldly. This week, we conclude our Bible study on prayer by looking at a prayer of Nehemiah when he was still in Persia after the Babylonian Captivity.

Some of the Jewish exiles had returned to Jerusalem after the Babylonian Captivity and rebuilt the temple. Almost eighty years later, a second group returned to start rebuilding the walls under Ezra's leadership, but they were stopped. Nehemiah heard about the situation in Jerusalem thirteen years after Ezra's expedition.[1] He boldly stepped forward in prayer and obedience to make a difference with his life.

Are we willing to step out and boldly ask God to use us for His kingdom?

THE SITUATION IN JERUSALEM

How do you respond when you hear bad news? With sadness? Anger? Helplessness? Or do you turn immediately to prayer? Nehemiah turned to prayer. Yes, he probably felt all the above emotions, but he turned to God when he received the discouraging news about the condition of Jerusalem and those who had returned after the captivity.

Nehemiah had a close relationship with God, as evidenced by the numerous references to prayer throughout this book. Today we're going to look at the situation that moved him to prayer. Let's pray for God to make us teachable.

> *Father, You want me to come to You in prayer when my world gets upset and life hurts, when I hear news that disturbs, when disappointments surround me. Teach me how to care for others the way Nehemiah did. I want to make a difference with my life like Nehemiah did. But am I committed to spending time in fervent prayer? Am I praying boldly? Am I willing to be used however You choose? Teach me, Lord, from Nehemiah's example.*

LOOKING TO GOD'S WORD
NEHEMIAH 1:1-4

1. When did Nehemiah receive this news about Jerusalem, and where was he at the time (v. 1)?[2]

2. How would you describe Nehemiah's heart? *X familiar question*

3. What is the situation in Jerusalem (v. 3)? Why would this cause Nehemiah great distress?

4. How does Nehemiah respond to the report given about the remnant in Judah (v. 4)? List all he did.

5. Why do you think he addresses his prayer to the "God of heaven" (vv. 4–5)? Which attribute of God does that name imply, and why would that attribute be comforting to Nehemiah at this point?

You might be wondering why Nehemiah was distressed by the news that the walls of Jerusalem weren't rebuilt. One Bible commentary explains: "In the ancient Middle East, a city wall provided protection for the inhabitants. The condition of a city wall was also seen as an indication of the strength of the people's gods. The ruined condition of the wall of Jerusalem reflected badly on God's name."[3]

LOOKING UPWARD

6. Describe a situation that disturbed you and moved you to fast and pray for a period of time. What were the results?

7. What are some alternatives people may turn to in distressing situations instead of turning to God in prayer?

8. What are some reasons why we wouldn't go to God in prayer in the middle of distressing news or circumstances?

LOOKING DEEPER

9. Ezra 1:1–4 gives us the background of the first remnant of Jews who returned to Jerusalem to rebuild the walls. What led Cyrus to allow the people to return according to verse 1?

10. What did he instruct them to do (vv. 2–3)?

11. How did Cyrus view God?

12. Describe his attitude toward the Jewish people.

LOOKING REFLECTIVELY

We often look around us and see things that distress us. It's hard to listen to the news without being disturbed by something that is happening in our city or nation or even the world. But how do we respond? Do we ignore what's going on because we feel as if we can't make a difference? Or do we pray, asking God how can we be involved in the solution? Nehemiah boldly stepped forward to lead the rebuilding of the wall of Jerusalem. He was willing to be used by God to make a difference.

Ukraine - stuff
Gaza - ?

X

How has God used you to make a difference in the lives of others?

When you hear disturbing news, are you willing to ask God how He might want to use you to be part of the solution? Spend some time praying about that now.

Nehemiah prayed for those in Jerusalem. Spend some time praying for others in tough situations today.

"O God, make us desperate, and grant us faith and boldness to approach Your throne and make our petitions known, knowing that in so doing we link arms with Omnipotence and become instruments of Your eternal purposes being fulfilled on this earth."[4]

NANCY DeMOSS WOLGEMUTH

HIS FOCUS ON GOD

Nehemiah faced a situation he knew he could not solve or fix by himself. But he also knew he served an omnipotent God. Today we're going to look at Nehemiah's prayer and the attitude with which he went before God. He didn't jump into prayer listing his requests, but he began by looking to his God. We would do well to follow his example.

> *Father, help me turn my focus to You before I begin to talk about my needs. When I begin with worship, You put everything into perspective and give me peace as I pray about those things on my heart. I bow my knees before You now and look to You.*

LOOKING TO GOD'S WORD
NEHEMIAH 1:5–11

1. Describe Nehemiah's prayer in Nehemiah 1:5–11.

read 4 & 6

2. Nehemiah began his prayer by focusing on God's attributes in verse 5. List all he says about God. Which attributes does he mention or refer to?

3. Why would these attributes be comforting at this time?

4. What words are repeated in his prayer? Why do you think he emphasized these words and phrases?

5. How long and how often did he pray, according to verses 4 and 6?

6. List the two cause and effect clauses God had spoken to Moses in verses 8–9. They read, "If . . . I will . . ."

7. Why do you think Nehemiah reminded God of His words to Moses?

LOOKING UPWARD

8. Nehemiah uses the word "beseech" twice in the NASB. It's translated "said" in the NIV and ESV. In verse 5, he begins his prayer, "I beseech You, O LORD God of heaven . . ." And he ends his prayer in verse 11, "O LORD, I beseech You . . ." When you hear the word "beseech," what do you think of? How would it differ from the word "said"?

LOOKING DEEPER

9. In Nehemiah 1:8–9, Nehemiah alluded to the message God gave Moses and the sons of Israel in Deuteronomy 30:1–10. As you read the Deuteronomy passage, what did Moses say would happen to them because of their disobedience?

10. What did God promise to do when they returned to the Lord and obeyed Him?

11. How would these promises motivate Nehemiah to pray for the situation in Jerusalem and for the people who had returned from captivity?

LOOKING REFLECTIVELY

Nehemiah was a prayer warrior. He heard about a situation that greatly distressed him, and he turned to God in prayer. He knew his God was big enough to do the difficult and seemingly impossible, and he wanted to be part of the solution. So he beseeched the Lord to use him. He was willing to step out in faith to encourage his brothers and sisters back in Jerusalem. The name Nehemiah means "The Lord has comforted."[5] What an appropriate name for this man.

- When have you beseeched the Lord about something? How did God work in your life through your prayer? How did God answer?
- Spend some time praising God for who He is, starting with His attributes mentioned in verse 5. Use Psalm 100 to guide you through a time of worship and prayer.

"The Old Testament saints didn't flippantly rush into God's presence, treating Him as if He were a man. They came before Him with reverence, recognizing that when they prayed they were coming face-to-face with Almighty God."[6]

JOHN MACARTHUR

HIS CONFESSION

Nehemiah began his prayer by focusing on God and His attributes. Now he turns his attention to confession of sins—not only his personally, but also those of the sons of Israel. He agreed with God that they had sinned, and he was specific about how they had displeased God. Nehemiah wanted to boldly come before God with his request, but he knew a clean heart was necessary in order to do this. Confession clears the way for us to come boldly into the presence of God as we acknowledge our sins and desire to turn away from them.

Lord, keep me sensitive to sins in my life so I may bring them before
You and confess them. Keep me from ignoring them or blaming them
on others. Thank You for Your forgiveness.

LOOKING TO GOD'S WORD
NEHEMIAH 1:5–11

1. Reread Nehemiah's prayer in Nehemiah 1:5–11. How would you outline his prayer?

2. What observations can you make about his confession in verses 6–7?

3. Why would he confess the sins of the sons of Israel and not just his own sins?

4. What was he confessing? What had they done?

LOOKING UPWARD

5. What moves you to confess sin?

6. What are some reasons why we would delay in confessing sins?

LOOKING DEEPER

Nehemiah 9 is a prayer of confession and thanks for God's faithfulness after the wall around Jerusalem was completed under Nehemiah's godly leadership. All the people gathered together. Ezra read the Book of the Law of Moses to them, and they were convicted of their sins. Nehemiah 9 records their prayer of confession.

7. As you read Nehemiah 9, how had the Israelites sinned against God (vv. 26–30, 33–35)?

8. How did God respond to the people each time they cried to Him (vv. 27–35)? On which attributes of God did they focus?

LOOKING REFLECTIVELY

There are times I've asked God, "Why do you love me? Especially after I've let you down in so many ways?" But God loves us unconditionally. His love isn't based on what we do or don't do. As we look back over our lives and make note of all God has done, it brings us to a place of confession and thankfulness. We confess as we recognize our sins, and we give thanks because God is faithful, even when we are not.

How have you seen His faithfulness in Your life? Write down some specific ways.

Write out Psalm 139:23–24 in your own words. Use David's words to guide you through a time of prayer and confession. Write your prayer below or in your prayer journal.

"Prayer honors God, acknowledges His being, exalts His power, adores His providence, secures His aid."[7]

E. M. BOUNDS

HIS REQUESTS

Nehemiah took time to worship God, focus on His attributes, and confess sins before he brought his requests to God. When we approach God in that way, we come to Him with a heart that delights in Him, and He delights in us. In Nehemiah 1:11, Nehemiah brings his requests before God. This is the shortest part of his prayer. Nehemiah gives us a great example of how to pray with boldness. We can pray for God to help us do the same.

Father, thank You for Your faithfulness to me. Thank You for never giving up on me, even when I disappoint You. Thank You for Your great mercy and forgiveness. Teach me as I remember Your work in the past to put my confidence in You for the future. Give me boldness to ask and confidence to wait on You to work, trusting Your hand for the answers.

LOOKING TO GOD'S WORD
NEHEMIAH 1:5-11

1. Reread Nehemiah's prayer in Nehemiah 1:5–11. What is his perspective of God in this prayer?

2. Why do you think he reminds God who the sons of Israel were in verse 10?

3. What does he ask of God in verse 11?

4. How does he refer to himself and the sons of Israel in verses 6, 10–11? Mark each time he uses this description in verses 5–11. What does that show us about his heart for God?

5. What does he mean when he asks God to make him "successful today"? Why would he ask that?

6. Why would he ask for compassion from the king?

At the end of verse 11, we learn Nehemiah's profession is the cupbearer to the king. As the king's cupbearer, Nehemiah was responsible for tasting the wine before serving it to the king to be sure it was not poisoned. As a result, he had frequent access to the king.[8] We may sometimes wonder why God has us in a certain place. God puts His people in the right places at the right time for His purpose.

LOOKING UPWARD

7. How have you seen God place you or someone else in the right place at the right time to help accomplish His purpose?

8. Nehemiah referred to God's promises in his prayer. What are some promises of God you are clinging to today?

enough gccc X

LOOKING DEEPER

9. Can you think of some biblical examples of God putting someone at the right place at the right time for His purpose? How did God use them? (For instance, Philip and the Ethiopian eunuch in Acts 8.)

LOOKING REFLECTIVELY

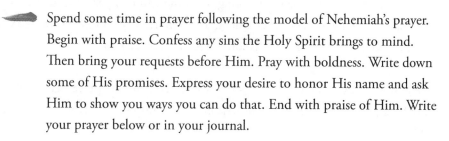 Spend some time in prayer following the model of Nehemiah's prayer. Begin with praise. Confess any sins the Holy Spirit brings to mind. Then bring your requests before Him. Pray with boldness. Write down some of His promises. Express your desire to honor His name and ask Him to show you ways you can do that. End with praise of Him. Write your prayer below or in your journal.

"Nehemiah did more than weep and pray; he made himself available to the Lord to get the job done. He depended on God's great power to work in and through him (Eph. 3:20–21). He was not content merely to get answers to prayer: he wanted to be an answer to prayer."[9]

WARREN WIERSBE

GOD'S ANSWER

Nehemiah was burdened to restore the walls and gates of Jerusalem, but he was still in Persia serving the king as his cupbearer. How could he be of any help? Still, Nehemiah stepped out in faith, boldly went before God in prayer, and asked God to grant him compassion before the king. Four months had passed since Nehemiah had received word about Jerusalem. The opportunity had finally come to go before the king and request permission to return to Jerusalem.

Today we're going to look at how God answered Nehemiah's prayer. Is there something you need to ask God for that may seem impossible? Don't limit God. Boldly ask.

Father, I confess I sometimes limit You by how I pray. If something seems impossible, I don't even approach You with it. Yet nothing is impossible with You. Teach me to ask You boldly for things that only You can do, things that would bring glory and honor to Your name.

LOOKING TO GOD'S WORD
NEHEMIAH 2:1-10

1. List your observations about Nehemiah from this passage. What stands out to you about him?

2. What are some possible reasons why Nehemiah had not made his request of the king before now?

3. The king noticed that Nehemiah was sad and asked why. Why would Nehemiah have been "very much afraid" (v. 2) when the king asked him about it?

4. How did Nehemiah respond to the king's question before he made his request?

5. In what ways can you see how Nehemiah had spent time preparing a plan before he asked the king to let him return to Judah?

LOOKING UPWARD

6. The king asked Nehemiah what he was requesting, and before he responded, Nehemiah "prayed to the God of heaven" (v. 4). Scripture doesn't record what he prayed, but what would you have prayed in this situation?

7. What are some principles from this chapter you can apply in your own life in the area of prayer?

LOOKING DEEPER

8. Nehemiah did return to Jerusalem and set out to do what was on his heart. Read Nehemiah 2:11–20 to see what happened when Nehemiah first got to Jerusalem. Describe how he assessed the damage to Jerusalem and the walls and gates (vv. 11–16).

9. What was his motivation behind rebuilding the wall of Jerusalem (v. 17)?

10. Describe the opposition he faced. How did he respond to it (vv. 19–20)?

LOOKING REFLECTIVELY

Nehemiah had a comfortable position working for the king. It would have been easy to ignore the situation in Jerusalem and go on with his life as it was. But Nehemiah would not settle for comfort and status quo while others were struggling in Jerusalem. God had laid on his heart to return to Judah and rebuild the city of Jerusalem. How could he not respond or at least try? He prayed and fasted before he made his request to the king, and the king granted his requests because "the good hand of my God was on me" (Neh. 2:8).

God answered his prayer with a *yes*. This was part of God's plan. But sometimes, God answers our prayers with a *no* or *not now*. The more time we spend alone with God, the more prepared we are for the way He chooses to answer our prayers. We don't know how Nehemiah might have responded had the king refused his request, but we do know he prayed fervently about this situation.

We can learn much from Nehemiah's example. Pray with boldness, ask God for great things only He can do, and trust God's sovereign hand in the way He answers.

- What do you need to boldly pray for today?
- What are some answers to prayer you have seen recently in your life or in the lives of others around you?
- Think through situations when God has not answered in the way you would have liked. Thank Him that He knows what He is doing. Choose to trust even though it may not make sense to you now.
- Nehemiah prayed passionately about what was on his heart. How can you deepen your prayer life? What needs to change?

Write a prayer of commitment to seek a deeper, more consistent—and bolder—prayer life.

_____

_____

_____

_____

_____

_____

_____

_____

_____

_____

"The goal of prayer is the ear of God. Prayer moves others through God's influence on them. It is not our prayer that moves people, but the God to whom we pray." [10]

J. OSWALD SANDERS

THE PRAYERS OF PROPHETS, WARRIORS, AND KINGS

I pray this study has taken your prayer life to a deeper level as you've learned from the prayers of these spiritual giants who have gone before us. We may not be prophets or kings, but we're all warriors as we fight spiritual battles every day. We can find victory in overwhelming situations as we turn to God in prayer. Prayer strengthens us when we're weak. We, too, can make an impact with our lives through prayer, just like the men and women we've spent the last eight weeks studying.

When you find yourself unsure of how to pray in a specific situation, revisit these prayers. Pray them in your own words and apply them to your unique situation. Pray like prophets, warriors, and kings—boldly praying prayers of eternal significance, heartfelt intercession, submission to God's will, supplication, lament, prayers for help, and prayers of worship.

WEEK 1 | JESUS: A MODEL PRAYER

"Pray, then, in this way: 'Our Father who is in heaven, Hallowed be Your name. Your kingdom come. Your will be done, On earth as it is in heaven. Give us this day our daily bread. And forgive us our debts, as we also have forgiven our debtors. And do not lead us into temptation, but deliver us from evil. [For Yours is the kingdom and the power and the glory forever. Amen.']" (Matt. 6:9–13)

WEEK 2 | PAUL: A PRAYER OF INTERCESSION

"For this reason I bow my knees before the Father, from whom every family in heaven and on earth derives its name, that He would grant you, according to the riches of His glory, to be strengthened with power through His Spirit in the inner man, so

that Christ may dwell in your hearts through faith; and that you, being rooted and grounded in love, may be able to comprehend with all the saints what is the breadth and length and height and depth, and to know the love of Christ which surpasses knowledge, that you may be filled up to all the fullness of God. Now to Him who is able to do far more abundantly beyond all that we ask or think, according to the power that works within us, to Him be the glory in the church and in Christ Jesus to all generations forever and ever. Amen." (Eph. 3:14–21)

WEEK 3 | JOB: A PRAYER OF DESPAIR

"Why is light given to him who suffers, And life to the bitter of soul, Who long for death, but there is none, And dig for it more than for hidden treasures, Who rejoice greatly, And exult when they find the grave? Why is light given to a man whose way is hidden, And whom God has hedged in? For my groaning comes at the sight of my food, And my cries pour out like water. For what I fear comes upon me, And what I dread befalls me. I am not at ease, nor am I quiet, And I am not at rest, but turmoil comes." (Job 3:20–26)

*Then Job answered the L*ORD *and said, "I know that You can do all things, And that no purpose of Yours can be thwarted. 'Who is this that hides counsel without knowledge?' Therefore I have declared that which I did not understand, Things too wonderful for me, which I did not know. 'Hear, now, and I will speak; I will ask You, and You instruct me.' I have heard of You by the hearing of the ear; But now my eye sees You; Therefore I retract, And I repent in dust and ashes."* (Job 42:1–6)

WEEK 4 | HANNAH: A PRAYER OF LONGING

*She, greatly distressed, prayed to the L*ORD *and wept bitterly. She made a vow and said, "O L*ORD *of hosts, if You will indeed look on the affliction of Your maidservant and remember me, and not forget Your maidservant, but will give Your maidservant a son, then I will give him to the L*ORD *all the days of his life, and a razor shall never come on his head."* (1 Sam. 1:10–11)

WEEK 5 | DAVID: A PRAYER OF LAMENT

"To You, O LORD, I lift up my soul. O my God, in You I trust, Do not let me be ashamed; Do not let my enemies exult over me. Indeed, none of those who wait for You will be ashamed; Those who deal treacherously without cause will be ashamed. Make me know Your ways, O LORD; Teach me Your paths. Lead me in Your truth and teach me, For You are the God of my salvation; For You I wait all the day. Remember, O LORD, Your compassion and Your lovingkindnesses, For they have been from of old. Do not remember the sins of my youth or my transgressions; According to Your lovingkindness remember me, For Your goodness' sake, O LORD. Good and upright is the LORD; Therefore He instructs sinners in the way. He leads the humble in justice, And He teaches the humble His way. All the paths of the LORD are lovingkindness and truth To those who keep His covenant and His testimonies. For Your name's sake, O LORD, Pardon my iniquity, for it is great. Who is the man who fears the LORD? He will instruct him in the way he should choose. His soul will abide in prosperity, And his descendants will inherit the land. The secret of the LORD is for those who fear Him, And He will make them know His covenant. My eyes are continually toward the LORD, For He will pluck my feet out of the net. Turn to me and be gracious to me, For I am lonely and afflicted. The troubles of my heart are enlarged; Bring me out of my distresses. Look upon my affliction and my trouble, And forgive all my sins. Look upon my enemies, for they are many, And they hate me with violent hatred. Guard my soul and deliver me; Do not let me be ashamed, for I take refuge in You. Let integrity and uprightness preserve me, For I wait for You. Redeem Israel, O God, Out of all his troubles." (Psalm 25)

WEEK 6 | ASA: A PRAYER OF SEEKING GOD

Then Asa called to the LORD his God and said, "LORD, there is no one besides You to help in the battle between the powerful and those who have no strength; so help us, O LORD our God, for we trust in You, and in Your name have come against this multitude. O LORD, You are our God; let not man prevail against You." (2 Chron. 14:11)

WEEK 7 | JEHOSHAPHAT: A PRAYER OF DEPENDENCE

"O LORD, the God of our fathers, are You not God in the heavens? And are You not ruler over all the kingdoms of the nations? Power and might are in Your hand so that no one can stand against You. Did You not, O our God, drive out the inhabitants of this land before Your people Israel and give it to the descendants of Abraham Your friend forever? They have lived in it, and have built You a sanctuary there for Your name, saying, 'Should evil come upon us, the sword, or judgment, or pestilence, or famine, we will stand before this house and before You (for Your name is in this house) and cry to You in our distress, and You will hear and deliver us.' Now behold, the sons of Ammon and Moab and Mount Seir, whom You did not let Israel invade when they came out of the land of Egypt (they turned aside from them and did not destroy them), see how they are rewarding us by coming to drive us out from Your possession which You have given us as an inheritance. O our God, will You not judge them? For we are powerless before this great multitude who are coming against us; nor do we know what to do, but our eyes are on You." (2 Chron. 20:6–12)

WEEK 8 | NEHEMIAH: A PRAYER OF BOLDNESS

"I beseech You, O LORD God of heaven, the great and awesome God, who preserves the covenant and lovingkindness for those who love Him and keep His commandments, let Your ear now be attentive and Your eyes open to hear the prayer of Your servant which I am praying before You now, day and night, on behalf of the sons of Israel Your servants, confessing the sins of the sons of Israel which we have sinned against You; I and my father's house have sinned. We have acted very corruptly against You and have not kept the commandments, nor the statutes, nor the ordinances which You commanded Your servant Moses. Remember the word which You commanded Your servant Moses, saying, 'If you are unfaithful I will scatter you among the peoples; but if you return to Me and keep My commandments and do them, though those of you who have been scattered were in the most remote part of the heavens, I will gather them from there and will bring them to the place where I have chosen to cause My name to dwell.' They are Your servants and Your people whom You redeemed by Your great power and by Your strong hand. O Lord, I beseech You, may Your ear be attentive to the prayer of Your servant and the prayer of Your servants who delight to revere Your name, and make Your servant successful today and grant him compassion before this man." (Neh. 1:5–11)

MORE PRAYERS FOR PRAYER WARRIORS

We weren't able to look at all the prayers in the Bible in these eight weeks, but I encourage you to study some of the other prayers on your own. To help you get started, I've listed some below. As you study them, look at the context before and after, and think through these questions:

1. What was the situation that led these people to pray? What motivated them to pray?
2. How did they approach God?
3. What did they include in their prayers?
4. What was the result of their prayers?
5. How did their relationship with God deepen as a result of their prayers?
6. How can you apply their prayers to your own life?

OTHER PRAYERS IN THE BIBLE:

Jacob: Genesis 32:9–12
Moses: Exodus 32:7–14; Deuteronomy 9:25–29
David: 1 Chronicles 29:10–19
Solomon: 1 Kings 3:6–9; 1 Kings 8:22–53
Elijah: 1 Kings 18:36–37
Hezekiah: 2 Kings 19:14–19; 2 Kings 20:1–7
Jeremiah: Jeremiah 32:16–25
Daniel: Daniel 9:1–19
Ezra: Ezra 9:5–15
Paul: Philippians 1:9–11

I'd love to hear how God has used this study to deepen your prayer life. You can reach me through my website at www.crickettkeeth.com. Take a look around, check out the other Bible studies I've written, and listen to some of the audio messages. My desire is to encourage others to passionately pursue Jesus Christ.

On bended knee with you,

Crickett

LEADER'S GUIDE

This study can be used individually, as well as with a small group. We used it in our women's ministry Bible study several years ago, and I gave the leaders direction each week with the questions before small group time. This guide is a result of that time with my small group leaders. Try to answer the questions on your own first, even if you're unsure how to answer. Then take a look at the guide to give you clarification and insight.

In your small groups, don't try to discuss every question for every day. Just pick three to four questions each day from the **Looking to God's Word** and **Looking Upward** sections, depending on how much time you have in small groups. Be sure to cover questions from all five days. I encourage you to circle the questions you'd like to ask as you first go through the study on your own. Which questions would promote rich discussion and help impart the main message of the lesson that day? I'll recommend questions in this guide, but feel free to use the questions you feel would be most helpful to your group.

The **Looking Deeper** questions cover other passages that enhance the study but aren't focused on the main passage of that day. In the small group times, I don't usually ask the **Looking Deeper** questions unless someone has a specific question about them.

Some of the **Looking to God's Word** questions are straightforward, and you're just answering directly from the passage. You don't need to ask those questions. Just summarize the answer (or ask someone in your small group to). Spend your time in small group focusing on the questions that are more open-ended and would best facilitate sharing and discussion.

In this Leader's Guide, I will point out the questions that would promote discussion, and I will also address some of the more challenging questions. You can also listen to the lectures for this study online (free downloads) on my website at www. crickettkeeth.com/media. They will be available fall 2019.

WEEK 1—JESUS: A MODEL PRAYER

DAY 1: WORSHIP

Have someone read Matthew 6:9–13.
Discuss questions 2, 4, 5, and 7.

2. What does the term *Father* imply? How should we respond to God as our Father?

We are His children and belong to Him. He cares for us. He protects, provides for, looks after, and loves us. We can find security and comfort in His love and know He is looking out for our good. So we can trust Him and rest in His love.

4. Why is it significant that He is in heaven?

He is our heavenly Father—sovereign, ruler, Creator, omniscient God. All who have placed their faith in the blood of Jesus Christ to pay the penalty for their sins can call Him Father, because He has adopted them into His family. But He is also personal and loving. He will take care of us. He knows what's best for us, and He lovingly gives us the best, even though it may not be what we want. When we acknowledge who He is, our Father, the God of heaven and earth, it gives us a proper perspective as we come to Him in prayer.

DAY 2: SURRENDER

Discuss questions 2, 4, 6, 7, and 8.

2. What does it mean to pray, "Your kingdom come"?

It means to pray for Him to return soon and establish His earthly kingdom when every knee will bow and He will rule over all. We also are to pray for Him to rule as King in our hearts today.

4. How does praying for His will to be done relate to praying for His kingdom to come? Why does He mention His will being done on earth as it is in heaven? What does this imply?

His will is that He would reign over His creation and every knee would bow. Even though some have surrendered to Him as Lord, the ultimate reign over all will come when He returns to set up His kingdom. His will is already being done in heaven. The angels submit and surrender to His will and yield to His sovereign reign.

6. How can we know God's will?

Look to His Word for the non-negotiables of His will. For those things that aren't clearly spelled out for us in the Bible, spend time in prayer seeking God's direction. Ask for wisdom from godly friends who know you and the situation well. Make sure you have no unconfessed sin so you can be attentive to the prompting of the Holy Spirit to guide you in making decisions.

7. Do our prayers change God's will or plan? Can they?

These are difficult questions, but it's important for us to wrestle with them and think them through. There is a tension here we have to live with. Can my prayers change God's will or plan? No, because God is sovereign and knows what He's going to do in His perfect plan, and He knows how He's going to bring it about. We can't improve God's plan. If we could control God, then He wouldn't be sovereign. However, God can use our prayers to change circumstances. He gives us the privilege of being part of His plan through our prayers. We know we are to pray (it's commanded throughout the Bible), and we also know God is sovereign.

8. If our prayers won't change God's will or plan, why pray?

God changes us as we pray, as He aligns our hearts to pray for His will. And when we pray according to God's will, He hears and answers us. R. C. Sproul answers these questions in this way: "But can our requests change God's sovereign plan? Of course not. When God sovereignly declares that he is going to do something, all of the prayers in the world aren't going to change God's mind. But God not only ordains ends, he also ordains means to those ends, and part of the process he uses to bring his sovereign will to pass are the prayers of his people. And so we are to pray."[1] We are to pray for God's will to be done. That doesn't mean we can't ask for what we want (Jesus did in the garden of Gethsemane), but we always need to acknowledge we want His will, not ours, to be done. We pray—asking for what God has laid on our hearts and allowing God to work in us as we pray—and then trust Him to accomplish His purpose and His will through our prayers.

DAY 3: SUPPLICATION

Discuss questions 2, 4, 6, 7, and 8.

6. If God knows what we need, why should we pray for it?

When we pray and ask God to meet our daily needs, we are acknowledging we need Him, and we're looking to Him to provide. It deepens our trust in Him as we acknowledge our dependence on Him. Prayer prepares us for the proper response to His answer. It delights Him that we are looking to Him as our provider instead of trying to do it on our own without Him.

8. Some Christians believe asking for God to address physical needs shows a lack of faith. How would you respond to that?

When we ask God to provide for our physical needs, we are acknowledging our trust in Him to provide in His way and timing.

DAY 4: CONFESSION AND FORGIVENESS

Discuss questions 2, 3, 5, and 7.

2. If Jesus forgave our sins through His death on the cross, why does He tell us to ask for forgiveness? What does He mean here?

He's not talking about the forgiveness we received at the cross. When we put our faith in Jesus and His payment for our sins, we were forgiven once and for all. Here He's talking about the ongoing confession each time we sin that restores broken fellowship with God.

3. and 5. "If you do not forgive others, then your Father will not forgive your transgressions."

If we truly understand God's forgiveness of us when we didn't deserve it, we should want to extend that same forgiveness to others who may not deserve it from our viewpoint. If we can't get to that point of forgiving others **over time**, we may not have accepted Jesus' payment for our sins, or we don't fully understand His forgiveness.

DAY 5: PROTECTION

Discuss questions 2, 7, 8, and 9.

2. What does Jesus mean when He tells us to pray, "Do not lead us into temptation"?

We are asking God to guide us so that we will not get out of His will and get involved in a situation of temptation or in a situation of tempting God so that He has to rescue us. We are asking Him to not permit us, through our weakness, to be led into temptation that is too much for us to stand against.

7. "Sanctify them in the truth." What is the truth? How does the truth sanctify us?

Sanctify means "to set apart for special use." The way God sanctifies us is through the truth of His Word.[2] As we read and apply God's Word in our lives, we are changed. We live to please God, not the world. As we allow God's Word to work in us, we become less like the world and more like Christ.

WEEK 2—PAUL: A PRAYER OF INTERCESSION

DAY 1: AN OVERVIEW OF PAUL'S PRAYER

Have someone read Paul's prayer in Ephesians 3:14–21.
Discuss questions 2, 4, and 5.

DAY 2: THE RELATIONSHIP WITH GOD

Discuss questions 1, 2, 4, and 5.

5. Does our posture in prayer matter to God?

Scripture doesn't indicate that any specific posture is necessary in prayer. Our posture—sitting, kneeling, lying face down, and bowing the head—isn't the important thing. Our heart attitude is what matters. We can still humble ourselves and revere God in any position. But when we kneel or bow our heads, we're demonstrating our humility and reverence for God in an outward manner.

DAY 3: THE REQUESTS (PART 1)

Summarize question 1.
Discuss questions 2, 3, 6, and 7.

3. What does Paul mean by "the inner man" in verse 16?

The "inner man" is the spiritual part of our nature, where the Holy Spirit dwells. It stands in contrast to our outer bodies, the flesh.

5. How many requests do you see in Paul's prayer?

Some say Paul only asked for one thing—that they would be strengthened in the inner man. Then he shares the results of that one request.[3] Others say he is making four requests, but they are all connected. The first request leads to the second request, which results in the third request, which then results in the fourth.[4] I lean toward the view that he is making two requests: that they would be strengthened by the Holy Spirit in them and that they would be able to know the love of Christ.[5]

DAY 4: THE REQUESTS (PART 2)

Discuss questions 2, 3, 6, and 8.

2. What does Paul mean when he prays that Christ may dwell in their hearts through faith?

He's praying for a lordship relationship. "Dwell" (*katoikēsai*) isn't referring to when Christ came to live within us at the moment of salvation. This word is used for permanent residence; it literally means "to settle down and be at home." So when Paul prays, "that Christ may dwell in your hearts through faith," he's praying that Christ may, literally, "be at home in" their hearts and that He would be at the very center of their lives. Once we turn our lives over to Him, He is able to settle down and feel at home (dwell in our hearts).[6]

6. What does it mean to be "filled up to all the fullness of God"? How does that happen in light of Ephesians 4:13?

It means to be all that God wants us to be; to become more like Christ each day.

8. Can a believer fully comprehend the love of Christ?

Not fully until we see Him face to face. The more we know Christ, the more there is to know.

DAY 5: THE BENEDICTION

Discuss questions 2, 3, 4, and 6.

WEEK 3—JOB: A PRAYER OF DESPAIR

DAY 1: A PRAYER OF TRUST

Summarize questions 1 and 3.
Discuss questions 2, 4, 5, 6, and 7. (You can combine questions 4 and 5.)

6. Why do you think God allowed Satan to test Job?

God knew Job's heart and how Job would grow closer to Him in the end. Perhaps He also wanted to show Satan just how strong Job's relationship with Him was.

7. How are we able to worship God in the middle of great loss as Job did?

We trust God's love for us and that He has a bigger purpose in this for our good. We draw from the power of the Holy Spirit within us to strengthen us and help us grow in our faith and trust in the way God is working. We keep our focus on God's character instead of our feelings.

DAY 2: PRAYERS OF LAMENT

Discuss questions 2, 4, 7, and 8.

8. How would you answer when someone asks you why they are suffering?

I was just recently asked this question. My answer was: I don't know why, but I know our God. I know He is a God of love, He is faithful, and He is sovereign. We have to trust His character even when we don't understand why. He knows the bigger picture.

DAY 3: SEEKING ANSWERS

Discuss questions 1, 3, 4, 5, 7, and 8. (You can combine questions 4 and 5.)

DAY 4: GOD'S RESPONSE

Discuss questions 2, 3, 5, and 7.
Under Looking Reflectively, ask participants what verses they wrote down that encourage them about God's character in hard times.

DAY 5: A PRAYER OF REPENTANCE

Discuss questions 1, 2, 3, 6, and 7.

WEEK 4—HANNAH: A PRAYER OF LONGING

DAY 1: THE SETTING

Have someone summarize the situation in this passage.
Discuss questions 2, 3, 4, 6, and maybe 7.

DAY 2: A PRAYER FROM THE HEART

Discuss questions 1, 7, 9, and 10.

9. Notice in verse 18 that when Hannah left, she ate and "her face was no longer sad." God had not answered her prayer, so why do you think her countenance changed?

She had done all she could do. She had poured out her heart to God, laying her request before Him. She had hope that God would answer.

10. Some have said Hannah was bargaining with God. Was she? Should we pray in this manner? Why or why not?

I don't think she was bargaining with God. Her motive for asking for a son wasn't to keep the gift for herself or flaunt him in Peninnah's face, but to give her son back to God to be used. We ask with pure motives, and we leave the answer in God's hands, trusting He knows what's best. We can't manipulate God.

DAY 3: THE ANSWER

Discuss questions 2, 3, 4, 5, and 6.

4. What do you think Elkanah meant in verse 23 when he said, "only may the LORD confirm His word"?

Elkanah accepted Hannah's decision to not accompany him to the family festival at Shiloh since Samuel wasn't yet weaned, but he wanted to see God bring about the fulfillment of Hannah's vow to give her son permanently to God as a Nazarite.[7]

5. Why would this be a good age to take Samuel to Eli?

He was still young enough that he wasn't too attached to his home. He was at a teachable age, and he was no longer dependent on his mother for food.

DAY 4: A PRAYER OF THANKSGIVING

Discuss questions 3, 4, 5, 8, and 9.

3. What does she mean by the phrase, "my horn is exalted in the LORD"?

"Horns, used by animals for defense and attack, symbolized strength. Thus Hannah spoke of her **horn** in describing the strength that had come to her because God had answered her prayer."[8]

DAY 5: MARY'S MAGNIFICAT

Discuss questions 2, 4, 5, and 6.

6. How was Hannah able to offer praise after giving up her beloved son for whom she had prayed? How are we able to offer praise when we have to let go of something or someone we cherish?

Just like Job and Hannah, we have to trust God as we give back to Him those things and people we cherish. We trust Him to meet our needs and longings through Him, and we trust His sovereignty over all things.

WEEK 5—DAVID: A PRAYER OF LAMENT

DAY 1: I LIFT UP MY SOUL

Have someone read all of Psalm 25. Summarize question 3.
Discuss questions 2, 4, and 6.

4. What does it mean to "lift up my soul" (v. 1)? How do we do that?

This "is an idiom used elsewhere to express deep longing, desire, and need."[9] We turn to God and cry out to Him, expressing our deep longings, desires, and needs.

DAY 2: MAKE ME KNOW YOUR WAYS

Discuss questions 1, 4, 5, 6, and 7.

DAY 3: PARDON MY SIN

Summarize question 6.
Discuss questions 1, 5, 7, and 8.

DAY 4: MY EYES ARE CONTINUALLY TOWARD THE LORD

Discuss questions 1, 3, 5, 6, and 7.

3. What does David mean by "the secret of the LORD" in verse 14?

Those who fear and revere the Lord pay attention and heed His Word. As a result, "they learn the secrets of God's wisdom."[10]

DAY 5: I TAKE REFUGE IN YOU

Discuss questions 1, 4, 5, and 6.
Ask if anyone would be willing to share their lament psalm. Don't force it, but offer the opportunity.

6. How would "integrity and uprightness" preserve us (v. 21)?

David is "asking God to show His righteousness by delivering the one who put his trust in Him."[11] God will take care of those who trust Him because God is good, righteous, and true to His promises.

WEEK 6—ASA: A PRAYER OF SEEKING GOD

DAY 1: THE SETTING

Have someone summarize questions 1–4.
Discuss questions 5, 6, 7, and 8.

DAY 2: THE PRAYER

Summarize question 1.
Discuss questions 2, 3, and 4.
Summarize questions 5, 6, and 7.
Depending on your group and time, you might ask for a volunteer to share their response to question 8.

DAY 3: THE EXHORTATION

Discuss questions 2, 3, 6, 7, and 8.

DAY 4: A TURNING POINT

Summarize question 1.
Discuss questions 2, 4, 5, 6, and 7.

DAY 5: ANOTHER PRAYER OF SEEKING GOD

Since this week's lesson is on Asa and his prayer, spend more time on the first four days. Ask question 7 to tie David's psalm to the story of Asa. (You could also ask question 6 if time allows.)

WEEK 7—JEHOSHAPHAT: A PRAYER OF DEPENDENCE

DAY 1: THE BEGINNING OF JEHOSHAPHAT'S REIGN

Discuss questions 2, 3, 4, and 6.

DAY 2: A DIFFICULT SITUATION

Discuss questions 2, 3, 4, and 7.

7. Jehoshaphat was afraid (v. 3). Are we sinning when we are afraid and fearful?

I don't think it's sin to feel fearful or afraid. But our response to that fear determines if it becomes sin or not. God commands us throughout the Bible to "fear not." Fear becomes sin when we let it paralyze us and keep us from following God's will and direction. It becomes sin when we look to others for protection and solutions instead of God. When the disciples were on the boat with Jesus during the storm in Matthew 8:23–27, Jesus asked them, "Why are you afraid, you men of little faith?" In that one question, Jesus pointed out the cause of our fear. We fear because we don't have faith that He is in control of every situation in our lives, that He is sovereign. We don't trust Him to do what's best for us. If we did, we wouldn't be afraid. (I have a series of blog posts about fear on my website at www.crickettkeeth.com.) Another verse you might refer to is 1 John 4:18—"There is no fear in love; but perfect love casts out fear."

DAY 3: THE DISCIPLINE OF FASTING

Summarize question 1.
Discuss questions 2, 3, 4, 5, and 6.

3. What was the purpose of sackcloth and ashes in fasting?

"Fasting, sackcloth, and dust were traditional signs of mourning."[12] In most of the situations in the Bible, they were outward signs to demonstrate confession and repentance, grief, or earnestness in their prayer to God for help.

4. How would fasting help us seek the Lord? How would it strengthen our prayers?

Fasting helps us listen to God more intently. When we fast and pray about a situation, we are expressing to God our earnest desire for Him to direct and guide in a situation. We focus and rely on Him for the strength, provision, and wisdom we need, in contrast to looking to other things that might satisfy or direct us. God often shows us sin we're weren't aware of, and as we're attentive and listening for His guidance, He draws us into a deeper intimacy with Him. When I feel hungry while fasting, it is a reminder that only God can fully satisfy my longings.

6. Does our fasting move God to answer our prayers in the way we desire?

No, because God is sovereign. We can't control His plans. However, fasting moves us more in line with God's will. We are more attentive to Him and willing to accept His answer. When I fast and pray, it helps me listen to God more intently, and my heart begins to desire His will more than my own.

DAY 4: JEHOSHAPHAT'S PRAYER

Discuss questions 1, 2, 4, and 5.

DAY 5: GOD'S ANSWER

Discuss questions 1, 2, 4, 6, and 7.

WEEK 8—NEHEMIAH: A PRAYER OF BOLDNESS

DAY 1: THE SITUATION IN JERUSALEM

Summarize questions 1, 3, and 4. Discuss questions 2, 5, 7, and 8.

DAY 2: HIS FOCUS ON GOD

Discuss questions 1, 2, 3, 7, and 8.

DAY 3: HIS CONFESSION

Discuss questions 2, 3, 5, and 6.

3. Why would Nehemiah confess the sins of the sons of Israel and not just his own?

They were one nation, all God's people. What one person did impacted the entire nation.

DAY 4: HIS REQUESTS

Discuss questions 2, 5, 6, 7, 8, and 9.

DAY 5: GOD'S ANSWER

Discuss questions 2, 3, 5, 6, and 7.

2. What are some possible reasons why Nehemiah had not made his request before now? (Four months had passed since he had received word of the situation in Jerusalem.)

Perhaps Nehemiah had been spending that time praying for the king's response and for guidance from God on the timing to talk to the king. He was probably waiting on God and not wanting to step out too soon on his own initiative.

3. The king noticed that Nehemiah was sad and asked why. Why would Nehemiah have been afraid when the king asked him about it?

There are several views on this. (1) He may have become concerned because he was suddenly aware that he had shown his private feelings and not kept them to himself, which was not proper etiquette for a servant. (2) The moment had finally come to broach the subject with the king, and he realized if he mishandled it, there probably wouldn't be another chance. (3) He would be asking the king to change his policy concerning Jerusalem. In Ezra 4:21, Artaxerxes had issued a decree "to make these men stop work, that this city may not be rebuilt until a decree is issued by me." Nehemiah would be asking a lot of the king, and if the king became angry, it would mean certain death.[13]

ACKNOWLEDGMENTS

My deepest gratitude to:

My small group Bible study at Northwest Bible Church in Dallas—for encouraging me to write my very first Bible study twenty years ago.

The women of the Heart to Heart Bible Study at First Evangelical Church in Memphis—for encouraging me to write the Bible studies each year and for serving as a test group for every study.

Sandra Glahn—for believing in me and mentoring me as a writer. You spurred me on to keep writing in times of discouragement. Thank you for investing in my life.

Carol Kent—for encouraging me to go to "one more conference" when I wanted to quit.

Judy Dunagan, my acquisitions editor and a kindred spirit—for believing in me and walking through this journey with me step by step. Thank you for your godly example and words of wisdom.

Amanda Cleary Eastep, my developmental editor—for your wisdom and guidance in the editing process and making this a far better study than what I started with.

Moody Publishers—for walking through every step of this process with me and making this dream a reality. You all are a delight to work with!

Susan Nelson, Mary Burgess, and Carol Newman—for proofing, editing, and giving valuable feedback on each Bible study I write.

My writing buddies—for spurring me on to keep writing and coming alongside me in so many ways, especially in prayer.

My mom, who's with her Savior now—for always pointing me to my Savior, Jesus Christ.

My family—for understanding when I had to pull away from family time to write.

My prayer warriors—without you, this work would not have been completed.

My church family at First Evangelical Church in Memphis—for encouraging me to use my gifts for God's glory and helping me develop as a writer and teacher.

Jesus—for drawing me to Yourself and giving me a passion to write for the purpose of drawing others closer to You.

NOTES

Praying Like Prophets, Warriors, and Kings: An Introduction

1. E. M. Bounds, *Purpose in Prayer* (Chicago: Moody, 1980), 40.

Week 1—Jesus: A Model Prayer

1. D. Martyn Lloyd-Jones, *Studies in the Sermon on the Mount* (Grand Rapids: Eerdmans, 1976), 301.

2. J. Oswald Sanders, *Prayer Power Unlimited* (Chicago: Moody, 1977), 106.

3. R. P. Martin, "Worship," in *The International Standard Bible Encyclopedia Revised*, G. W. Bromiley, ed. (Grand Rapids: Eerdmans, 1979–1988), Vol. 4, 1118.

4. Nancy DeMoss Wolgemuth, *The Quiet Place: Daily Devotional Readings* (Chicago: Moody, 2012), Dec. 3.

5. John MacArthur, *Matthew 1–7*, The MacArthur New Testament Commentary series (Chicago: Moody, 1985), 379, emphasis added.

6. Judson W. Van De Venter, "I Surrender All," Timeless Truths, 1896, https://library.timelesstruths.org/music/I_Surrender_All/.

7. Charles Spurgeon, *The Power of Prayer in a Believer's Life*, Robert Hall, ed. (Lynnwood, WA: Emerald Books, 1993), 109–10.

8. Arthur W. Pink, *The Sovereignty of God* (Blacksburg, VA: Wilder Publications, 2008), 137.

9. Dwight L. Moody and S. G. Hardman, *Thoughts for the Quiet Hour* (Willow Grove, PA: Woodlawn Electronic Publishing, 1998), June 3.

10. Edwin A. Blum, "John," in *The Bible Knowledge Commentary: An Exposition of the Scriptures,* John F. Walvoord & R. B. Zuck, eds. (Wheaton, IL: Victor Books, 1985), Vol. 2, 333.

11. The *ESV Study Bible* explains: "'For yours is the kingdom and the power and the glory, forever. Amen'" is evidently a later scribal addition, since the most reliable and oldest Greek manuscripts all lack these words, which is the reason why these words are omitted from most modern translations. However, there is nothing theologically incorrect about the wording (cf. 1 Chron. 29:11–13), nor is it inappropriate to include these words in public prayers." See the *ESV Study Bible* (Wheaton, IL: Crossway Bibles, 2008), 1832.

12. Arthur Bennett, ed., *The Valley of Vision: A Collection of Puritan Prayers and Devotions* (Carlisle, PA: The Banner of Truth Trust, 1975), 182.

Week 2—Paul: A Prayer of Intercession

1. E. M. Bounds, *Power Through Prayer* (Minneapolis: World Wide Publications, 1989), 36.

2. Lloyd John Ogilvie, *You Can Pray with Power* (Ventura, CA: Regal, 1988), 28.

3. Andrew Murray, *The Prayer Life* (Chicago: Moody, 2013), 17–18.

4. Anna B. Warner, "Jesus Loves Me" (Words and Music: Public Domain), https://hymnary .org/text/jesus_loves_me_this_i_know_for_the_bible.

5. John Piper, *Let the Nations Be Glad!: The Supremacy of God in Missions* (Ada, MI: Baker Academic, 2010), 79.

6. Andrew Murray, *Waiting on God* (New Kensington, PA: Whitaker House, 1983), 24.

Week 3—Job: A Prayer of Despair

1. Wolgemuth, *The Quiet Place*, July 11.

2. Philip Yancey, *Disappointment with God: Three Questions No One Asks Aloud* (Grand Rapids: Zondervan, 1988), 207.

3. Thomas L. Constable, "Job," in *the Expository Notes of Dr. Thomas L. Constable* (CD Rom, 2008), 27.

4. Carol Kent, *When I Lay My Isaac Down: Unshakable Faith in Unthinkable Circumstances* (Colorado Springs: NavPress, 2013), 72.

5. Andrew Murray, *Waiting on God* (New Kensington, PA: Whitaker House, 1983), 24.

6. Ogilvie, *You Can Pray with Power*, 92.

Week 4—Hannah: A Prayer of Longing

1. John MacArthur, *The MacArthur Study Bible* (Nashville: Thomas Nelson, 2006), 371.

2. Vickie Kraft, *Facing Your Feelings* (Dallas: Word, 1996), 254–55.

3. Thomas L. Constable, *Tom Constable's Expository Notes on the Bible* (Garland, TX: Galaxie Software, 2003), 1 Samuel 1:9.

4. George Bowen, in *Thoughts for the Quiet Hour*, ed. D. L. Moody (Chicago: Moody Press, 1941), 50.

5. W. O. Neely, "1 Samuel," in *The Moody Bible Commentary*, Michael Rydelnik and Michael Vanlaningham, gen. eds. (Chicago: Moody, 2014), 405.

6. Matthew Henry, *Matthew Henry's Commentary on the Whole Bible*, vol. 2 (Iowa Falls, IA: Riverside, 1983), 248.

7. Hannah Whitall Smith, *The Christian's Secret of a Happy Life* (Ada, MI: Revell, 2012), 187–88.

Week 5—David: A Prayer of Lament

1. Harriet Hill et al., *Healing the Wounds of Trauma: How the Church Can Help*, North America Edition (New York: American Bible Society, 2014), 41.

2. Bennett, *The Valley of Vision*, 231.

3. Amy Carmichael, *Gold Cord: The Story of A Fellowship* (Fort Washington, PA: Christian Literature Crusade, 1998), 65.

4. Bennett, *The Valley of Vision*, 146.

5. Lawrence O. Richards, *The Bible Reader's Companion*, electronic ed. (Wheaton, IL: Victor Books, 1991), 356.

6. Mary DeMuth, *Jesus Every Day: A Journey Through the Bible in One Year* (Eugene, OR: Harvest House, 2018), 115.

Week 6—Asa: A Prayer of Seeking God

1. Allen C. Myers, *The Eerdmans Bible Dictionary* (Grand Rapids: Eerdmans, 1987), 486.

2. Timothy Keller, *Counterfeit Gods* (New York: Riverhead Books, 2009), xix.

3. C. Samuel Storms, *Reaching God's Ear* (Wheaton, IL: Tyndale, 1988), 23.

4. Andrew E. Hill, "1 & 2 Chronicles," in *The NIV Application Commentary* (Grand Rapids: Zondervan, 2003), 473.

5. John Piper, "What Does It Mean to Seek the Lord?," Desiring God, August 19, 2009, https://www.desiringgod.org/articles/what-does-it-mean-to-seek-the-lord.

6. Cynthia Heald, *Becoming a Woman of Prayer* (Colorado Springs: NavPress, 2005), 14.

7. William W. Walford, "Sweet Hour of Prayer," 1845, https://hymnary.org/text/sweet_hour_of_prayer_sweet_hour_of_pray.

8. Jan Winebrenner, *Intimate Faith: A Woman's Guide to the Spiritual Disciplines* (New York: Warner, 2003), 146.

Week 7—Jehoshaphat: A Prayer of Dependence

1. Benjamin Jenks, *Prayers Across the Centuries* (Wheaton, IL: Harold Shaw, 1993), 99.

2. W. Glyn Evans, *Daily with the King* (Chicago: Moody, 1979), 188.

3. Donald Whitney, *Spiritual Disciplines for the Christian Life* (Colorado Springs: NavPress, 1991), 157.

4. Pink, *The Sovereignty of God*, 141.

Week 8—Nehemiah: A Prayer of Boldness

1. William MacDonald, *Believer's Bible Commentary* (Nashville: Thomas Nelson, 1995), 482.

2. The month Chislev is equivalent to our mid-November to mid-December. The twentieth year refers to the twentieth year of Artaxerxes as king over the Persian Empire. Susa was the capital and the home of the king's winter palace. Most of the Jews had returned to Judah, but Nehemiah stayed behind in Persia and was serving the king as his cupbearer. See Warren Wiersbe's book *Be Determined* (Wheaton, IL: Victor Books, 1996), 14.

3. Earl Radmacher et al., *Nelson's New Illustrated Bible Commentary* (Nashville: Thomas Nelson Publishers, 1999), 584.

4. Nancy DeMoss Wolgemuth, *A Place of Quiet Rest: Finding Intimacy with God Through a Daily Devotional Life* (Chicago: Moody, 2000), 246.

5. Wiersbe, *Be Determined*, 14.

6. John MacArthur, *Alone with God: The Power and Passion of Prayer* (Wheaton, IL: Victor Books, 1995), 32.

7. E. M. Bounds, *The Complete Works of E. M. Bounds on Prayer: Experience the Wonders of God through Prayer* (Ada, MI: Baker Books, 2004), 338.

8. Gene Getz, "Nehemiah," in *The Bible Knowledge Commentary*, 675.

9. Warren Wiersbe, *With the Word Bible Commentary* (Nashville: Thomas Nelson, 1991), Neh. 1:1.

10. J. Oswald Sanders, *Spiritual Leadership* (Chicago: Moody, 2007), 90.

Leader's Guide

1. R. C. Sproul, *Now That's a Good Question!* (Wheaton, IL: Tyndale House, 2001), 200.

2. Blum, "John," in *The Bible Knowledge Commentary*, 333.

3. Harold W. Hoehner, "Ephesians," in *The Bible Knowledge Commentary*, 631.

4. Warren Wiersbe, *The Bible Exposition Commentary*, vol. 2 (Wheaton, IL: Victor Books, 1996), 31.

5. G. W. Peterman, "Ephesians," in *The Moody Bible Commentary*, 1851.

6. Hoehner, "Ephesians," in *The Bible Knowledge Commentary*, 631.

7. Ralph W. Klein, "1 Samuel," in *Word Biblical Commentary*, vol. 10 (Dallas: Word, 1998), 10.

8. Eugene H. Merrill, "1 Samuel," in *The Bible Knowledge Commentary*, vol. 1 (Wheaton, IL: Victor Books, 1985), 434.

9. Michael Rydelnik et al., "Psalms," in *The Moody Bible Commentary*, 783.

10. Radmacher, *Nelson's New Illustrated Bible Commentary*, 665.

11. MacDonald, *Believer's Bible Commentary: Old and New Testaments*, 584.

12. Radmacher, *Nelson's New Illustrated Bible Commentary*, 595.

13. Derek Kidner, *Ezra and Nehemiah: An Introduction and Commentary*, vol. 12 (Downers Grove, IL: InterVarsity Press, 1979), 87.

The everlasting truth of our great salvation

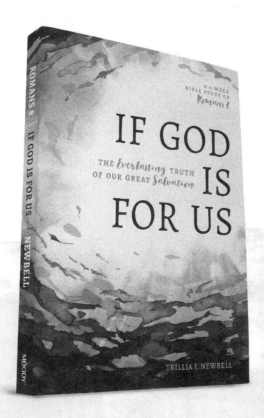

In this 6-week study, Trillia Newbell will walk you through Romans 8 and help you internalize the scandalous truths of our great salvation, our inheritance, the assurance of our faith, and ultimately the love of our good Father.

978-0-8024-1713-8　|　also available as an eBook

Do you long for a faith that moves mountains?

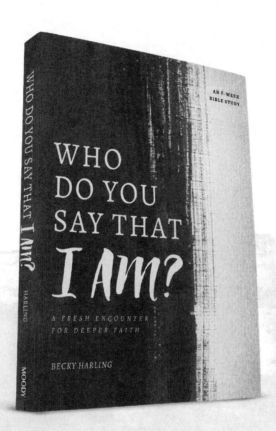

This study in the "I AM" statements of Jesus will help women move from knowing about Him to knowing Him personally. *Who Do You Say that I AM?* will draw women deep into the Word for a true encounter with Christ, helping them become more confident, calm, and courageous in the faith.

978-0-8024-1550-9 | 978-0-8024-1879-1 DVD | also available as an eBook

MOODY Publishers®

From the Word to Life®

Bible Studies for Women

IN-DEPTH. CHRIST-CENTERED. REAL IMPACT.

AN UNEXPLAINABLE LIFE
978-0-8024-1473-1

THE UNEXPLAINABLE CHURCH
978-0-8024-1742-8

HIS LAST WORDS
978-0-8024-1467-0

I AM FOUND
978-0-8024-1468-7

INCLUDED IN CHRIST
978-0-8024-1591-2

THIS I KNOW
978-0-8024-1596-7

WHO DO YOU SAY THAT I AM?
978-0-8024-1550-9

HE IS ENOUGH
978-0-8024-1686-5

IF GOD IS FOR US
978-0-8024-1713-8

UNEXPLAINABLE JESUS
978-0-8024-1909-5

MOODY Publishers®

From the Word to Life®

Explore our Bible studies at
moodypublisherswomen.com

Also available as eBooks